Christ's Life: Our Life

Christ's Life: Our Life

John B. Coburn

A Crossroad Book
The Seabury Press / New York

1978
The Seabury Press
815 Second Ave., New York, N.Y. 10017

Library of Congress Cataloging in Publication Data

Coburn, John B   Christ's life—our life.
"A Crossroad book."
1. Jesus Christ—Biography—Devotional literature. 2. Christian biog-
raphy—Palestine. 3. Identification (Religion) I. Title.
BT306.5.C63   232.9′01 [B]   77-17172
ISBN 0-8164-0384-8   ISBN 0-8164-2616-3

All quotations from the Bible are from the Revised Standard Version,
copyright 1946 and 1952 by Division of Christian Education of the National
Council of Churches of Christ in the United States of America.

Dedication

The first time I used the phrase "The Story of Jesus—and Our Story" (which has been somewhat shortened for publication purposes), was as the title of an ecumenical series of lectures—the J. Richard and Elsie Smith Pierce Christian Lectures—given at the First United Methodist Church in Pine Bluff, Arkansas in October 1973. Since then I have revised the original series so many times that there is little resemblance between what was said then and what appears in this book. The theme, however, has remained the same and the more changes rung upon it the more clear, it seems to me, is the relationship between the story of Jesus and the story of our own individual lives.

The Pierce Lectures are given annually as a memorial to J. Richard and Elsie Smith Pierce, endowed by a gift from their son, Dr. J. Richard Pierce, Jr., and daughter-in-law, Bettie Mildred Pierce. I wish therefore to dedicate this book to Dr. and Mrs. J. Richard Pierce, Jr. and thus to the laypersons of whatever religious persuasion who, by the story of their own lives in each generation, bear witness to the eternal story of Jesus in every age.

Duneloch   *John B. Coburn*
Wellfleet, Massachusetts
August, 1977

AN ACKNOWLEDGMENT

I wish to acknowledge with deep appreciation the editorial help of Robert Gilday, without whose encouragement these talks would not have been published and who has helped shape their present form with his professional and personal concern. As always, I am indebted to Patricia Nason, my administrative assistant and friend of many years, for her perceptive eye and judgment as well as for her superb typing. To Sheila Hard, who carried an extra secretarial load, I am also most grateful.

Contents

Introduction

We human beings tend to separate ourselves from God by following our own wills. Fortunately, he has not let us go our own ways but continually seeks to be at one with us. The truth is that we are one with him—though this is not always evident from our behavior, nor even at times our wishes. That truth has been made clear in the life of Jesus Christ, and the evidence revealed in the story of his life, which includes his death and resurrection.

As we go about writing the story of our individual lives, we are helped to write that story in accordance with the truth that God is at one with us. That is to say, to write the true story of our lives we must read his story, and also be sensitive to that which rises within us so that we can read intelligently what is happening to us. We find our story unfolding by looking both at him as his story is told in the Bible and by looking within ourselves.

So we shall try to keep both of these stories before us as we proceed, remembering that while we can read his story with our outward eyes, we can write our own stories only as we live them. And we shall come, we pray, at the end to realize that his story was not completed in New Testament times but continues to be written in our lives. The miracle is, that he wants us to write it.

1

His Birth

Let us go back to the beginning—at least to the beginning as it was written by St. Mark in the earliest of the four Gospel narratives. Mark's story begins like this:

> The beginning of the gospel of Jesus Christ, the Son of God. As it is written in Isaiah the Prophet, "Behold, I send my messenger before thy face, who shall prepare thy way." (Mark 1:1–2)

So the story really begins before Jesus' birth. It is anticipated in the Old Testament, and begins in fact at the beginning of time, indeed before time, before the foundations of the world were built, in the mind of God himself. When history began at the dawn of human consciousness and people began to deal with the mystery of human existence, they struggled to probe that mystery by telling primitive stories—like the story of the Garden of Eden, and Adam and Eve, and the Serpent. The Jewish people saw their history to be one which would try to explain this mystery for all people. So they dealt with such human problems as hunger and slavery, justice and injustice, morality and immorality, by trying to discover what God was doing through them. They were, they believed, living out in a unique way what was in God's mind from the very beginning of time. In this tradition Isaiah, one of their prophets, said he looked forward to a time when God would send a special messenger—John the Baptist—to prepare the way of the Lord; that is, to help the Jewish people get ready for the coming of Jesus. So Mark begins his story.

Jesus Christ was born in the year 4 B.C. and died in the year 28 A.D., give or take one or two years. He was brought up in a middle-class artisan family in Nazareth, a small town in a province of the Roman Empire, Galilee.

The only recorded incident of the growing-up years was a pilgrimage that he took with his parents on one of the High Holy days of the Jewish faith to pray in the Temple in Jerusalem.

At about the age of thirty, he began to go around the countryside from town to town talking about the coming Kingdom of God, explaining what he thought its nature to be, teaching the reality of God expressed in that Kingdom, and its effect upon men and women who are living their lives on earth. He drew about him in a particularly close relationship twelve men who became his disciples and to whom he revealed his innermost thoughts.

He did this for approximately three years. As he described the reality of God as he knew it, he increasingly earned the enmity of the religious leaders, who considered his teaching blasphemy, and the suspicion of the political leaders. Finally the enmity and the suspicion became so great that he was accused of both blasphemy and treason and put to death in Jerusalem. Jesus had already anticipated this death and had tried to prepare his disciples for it by saying that, after he had been put to death, he would be raised from the dead and that they were, therefore, to trust him and not to be afraid of anything that might happen to him—or to them.

In the days following his death, first the disciples and then gradually an increasing number of people—in excess of five hundred—became convinced that he had in fact been raised from the dead, that he had spoken the truth, that he was alive. They experienced his presence. What he had said *would* come to pass, *had* come to pass. It was after the resurrection that they came to trust him. They gradually began to see that there was nothing they ever had to fear anymore—not even their deaths. Nobody, when they really trusted him, could do anything to them that would destroy them.

As they tried to describe to those who had not known Jesus the exact quality of this experience, the words that they came to use most frequently were, "Jesus is Lord." He is in charge. The reality of the universe is expressed in him. God and his Kingdom are the reality with which we have to reckon for the rest of our lives. The way to reckon with that reality is to trust him. They said, "Trust him; you will find him trustworthy. In that trust you will find your life."

In varying degrees that has been the experience of Christians for two thousand years, including the experience of many of you who are reading this book.

We write, therefore, this story of Jesus Christ—from his birth to his resurrection—in order that the knowledge of him that you already have may be deepened; and if you do not have much knowledge, or even any knowledge, that it may at least be begun. The purpose of this book is that we might *know* him; so that the experience of the first-century Christians may become in some measure our experience in the twentieth century.

To come to this knowledge we shall use two sources:

one is the story told by his disciples and those who directly followed them for approximately one hundred years after the resurrection. We shall try to get inside the knowledge that they had of Jesus Christ as they explained it. That explanation is in the New Testament. That is one source: the story *they* tell. We shall listen to them.

The other source is *ourselves*. Knowledge of Jesus Christ is always a personal knowledge. It is a knowledge that arises out of his presence now among us and within us as we trust him. In that respect, it is exactly the same today as it was then—no difference whatsoever. So we shall listen, not only to the disciples, but also to ourselves to hear the same story (as the hymn has it) "of Jesus and his love." We shall learn from our life together and our own inner lives.

We begin, as all stories should, at the beginning, with his birth. But we discover that his birth is *not* the beginning. The beginning, say the authors of the New Testament, was not when Jesus was born in Bethlehem, but rather when the world was born. That is where Christ has been since before the beginning. The disciples said, "When we saw him as a man we saw in him the power that had been from the beginning of all creation. He is the power behind the process of evolution when it started and has been involved in that process ever since. That is the one we lived with."

He was born just at the right time so he could be himself. He was born, they said, "in the fulness of time" to reveal the character of the universe, of God. Before his birth, a period of preparation went on for billions of years. Mankind had to be prepared by millions of years of evolving out of nothing finally into *homo sapiens*—a created being who had a mind and could think, who came to recognize the difference between right and wrong and had to decide between the two, emerged finally from his tribal life in the caves, from a nomadic life, to a pastoral agricultural life, to an urban life. All the laws developed by the societies of men to hold people together in some kind of a rough justice, and all the visions men had of what justice might become and how people might live together in harmony, all those visions expressed by poets and prophets—these were summed up in the One who was the law and the prophets, a Jew who had a special gift of wrestling with eternal meaning and the mystery of human existence. It was as a member of the Jewish race that he came to be born at a particular time which was "the fulness of time."

He came to a particular people for all mankind. He came as Man (with a capital *M*). He had two characteristics as Man: reality and compassion, truth and love. He came as the foundation of the world expressed in love. He came as God and Man. All together: the particular and the universal, the earthly and the eternal, the human and the divine.

This is the story the disciples are trying to tell—the story of how the immortal, invisible, all-powerful God came to earth to live a mortal, visible, powerless life as a baby. In Jesus they met the reality of God so that they could say, "The truth of existence is that compassion is more powerful than anything else—more powerful than even your sin or your death. Trust that compassionate, graceful love which you experience in your own lives. Trust it. Live it. That is to participate in eternal life because that is the way eternity is. You already have it. It is right here. You don't have to do anything to earn it or to get it. It is given. What you have was most uniquely given in Jesus Christ."

When they presented the story of Jesus, they did not refer so much to what his teachings were or what he did; they presented *him*. They did not so much urge their hearers to imitate him and to become good people, as to trust him and who he was. His message, in other words, was *himself*.

The question, then: What did he think of himself? How did he consider that self? Who did he think he was?

The uniqueness of Jesus consisted in the consciousness of an utterly unique relationship with God. The relationship was that of a son to a father. "No one knows the father," he says, "except his son. No one knows the son except the father. The knowledge of God that I have is the unique knowledge that a son has of a father, and I am going to give that knowledge to those who trust me. If you trust me, you will know."

How he came to that knowledge and how we come to the knowledge of ourselves, we shall learn as we go on.

> *Lord, Jesus, when we know you a little bit, we trust you a little bit.*
>
> *We thank you for the little knowledge you have given us. We hope we may trust you more and more.*
>
> *Help us to know you day by day as we trust you, so that you may give us more of yourself.*
>
> *Amen.*

2

His Baptism

We ended the last chapter with these questions: What did Jesus think of himself? How did he consider himself? Who did he think he was?

To find help in answering these questions we turn to the account of his baptism.

> In those days Jesus came from Nazareth of Galilee and was baptized by John in the Jordan. And when he came up out of the water, immediately he saw the heavens opened and the Spirit descending upon him like a dove; and a voice came from heaven, "Thou art my beloved Son; with thee I am well pleased." (Mark 1:9–11)

He came to himself at his baptism—he knew who he was uniquely. His uniqueness was that relationship of a son to a father. It was through his baptism that he discovered his unique self.

So when we begin to reflect upon who we are, we too can begin with our baptism. It is there we are named "John" or "Mary" by those who speak for God in the company of the people of God and are identified uniquely. There is no one who is precisely as we are. No one can give to the world what we can. No other can be ourselves. So we begin with our uniqueness. As Jesus came in the fullness of time for his unique self to be revealed, we come in our own particular fullness of time for our unique selves to be revealed. This is the time, the only time, the fullness of time.

So Christ accepted his time, the circumstances of his time, the people of his time. He did not wish for another time, nor another set of circumstances, nor different people, different social structures, a different place. Since his time was the only time for the uniqueness of himself to be, he accepted his time.

So *acceptance* is a key to our understanding of ourselves, coming to understand our unique selves. We often think we can only become ourselves by changing ourselves, or changing others, or wishing for different circumstances or another time. We seek fulfillment for another time—in the future or sometimes in the past. Baptism means first of all accepting life just as it is. It means accepting ourselves just as we are, where we are, with all relationships just as they are. It means accepting all the people in those relationships just as they are. They are unique selves and they are loved by God just as he loves us.

Jesus was *immersed* in the river Jordan. He went all the way down—down into his history, the history of his people, down into their sin and weakness, down into the depths of their lives. He took upon himself the hands of John and John's preaching the baptism of repentance for the forgiveness of sins. Jesus identified himself with his people. He did not stand off; he went down with them. He took for himself all their sins as well as their righteousness. He was willing to let his people tell him who he was—or rather, it was only as he accepted them, identified with them, that he heard inwardly (nobody heard it) the declaration that he was a beloved son in whom his father was well pleased. He discovered himself through his people. It means acceptance, immersion and going down with them.

And he had to *trust* himself in the hands of John.

The parallel is not difficult to make. We come to our identities as we accept them for our accepting those we belong to, identifying with them, being immersed with them. When a person cannot affirm himself, perhaps others can. A birthday party affirms a young child, lets him know he is someone special. You are pleased that he is. The church affirms this through baptism, through people. To be baptized is to be immersed and to trust that when you emerge from the waters—from the fear of losing control of your life, from the pain of immersion—you will have a clearer idea of who you are under God. Your unique self is matured through such acts of decision that you will go ahead, purified as it may be.

Christ came to his understanding of who he was and we come to our understanding of who we are by a fundamental decision at certain turning points in our lives to trust somebody else, to trust some other people, to deliberately involve ourselves with them. As we let them carry us, we let God tell us who we are.

God usually speaks to us through the pressure points of our lives. He deals with people as he sees fit to deal with them. But it seems fair to say at those decisive turning points, where we are forced to make decisions about life because there is not other option open to us, that he comes to help us discover who we are and who he is calling us to be.

The inner pressure in Jesus' life of trying to discover who he was had been building for thirty years. Who was he during those years known as the "hidden years" as he matured? What was he called upon by God to do?

How was he going to know in his own person the absolute reality of God on earth? How could he give his
unique expression of his knowledge of God? He had to
make a decision just the way you and I have to make a
decision when pressure has built up and we come to
turning points. His decision at his baptism was to cast
his lot with the people, to be involved in their lives; to
trust them, finally, with his life. It was as they handled
him, not as he handled them, as they dealt with him
and finally crucified him that God through his resurrection showed who he was—his beloved son. He showed
that to the world. Jesus came to know himself through
those other people.

Where are the pressure points in your life today?
Where are you being forced to make certain fundamental decisions? Where are you being drawn beyond yourself? Where are you going if you are going to move and
be more creative, more free, more affirmative, more
yourself? What decisions are being pressed upon you?
Where are you in your life both frightened and fas-
cinated at the same time? What part of your life
presents itself as an aspect of your life that you have got
to do something about? That is probably where God is
calling you to become more yourself.

If you are to become more yourself—under him—the
way to do it will be as you decide to go toward someone
or some ones, to be willing to be more, rather than less,
in touch, more identified with them, more involved,
more trusting, more willing to let them have their way
with you rather than you having your way with them. It
is exactly the opposite of cutting yourself off, of with-
drawing, of moving into more and more isolation, or
moving into people's lives only to control them.

You want to go out to people to serve them? Perhaps
the best way to do something for another person is to let
that person do something for you. You want to help

him? Tell him *you* need help. You want to strengthen another human being? Ask him to listen to you while you tell him about your pressures.

When you are under pressure, often the best way to proceed is to let another person do something for you, perhaps no more than listen. The point is you go toward another, not withdraw into yourself.

Where are those pressures? Only you can define them in your own life. They can be anywhere—in family life, in personal life, in professional life; with people we like, people we dislike, people we have responsibilities for, people for whom we have no responsibilities; an uneasy conscience about our national life, our political life, our church life.

As we become older, there is a built-in sense of becoming more cut off. That is a terribly excruciating pressure point. When that happens we have to decide who God is calling us to be toward the end of our life just as much as at the beginning. He is always calling us toward *more* life, a deeper knowledge of ourselves. He never calls us into self-pity or self-indulgence or sulking; into nothing but grieving or licking our wounds in life. He calls us always to acceptance of pain as glory, to death as to birth, to deeper hopes and relationships with those around us, to greater expectancy of what life is meant to be for us and of who we yet may become. It is never-ending, this outgoing trust, even beyond the grave into a new resurrected life. The key is the same: going toward, trusting, affirming others, affirming even—especially—the pressure points. Then one day we will learn who we *really* are.

How do you become who you are? As you trust yourself, your fellow man, and your God. They will tell you who you are as you make your decisions to go toward them in trust, to be immersed, to be involved.

Christ is in that immersion with you. Christ is in

those people. He is immersed in the waters and the turmoil, in the pain and the difficult decisions, in all the struggles. He is there with you in that kind of immersion. He is also in the opening of the heavens when you see the vision of who you are and who you are to become. He is the voice that you hear: You are my beloved. That is really who you are. I like you. I love you.

Let us not worry too much about who is for us or agrees with us, or who is against us and disagrees. Let us not worry too much about who understands us or who turns his back. Rather, may we see to it that in everything we do, we do it with Christ and in his spirit.

> Lord Jesus, we know we cannot understand everything about you, or about ourselves. But we do know that we come to know ourselves best as we trust you. You are trustworthy; whatever you say you will do, you do. Help us then to trust you more and more each day, to keep an eye on you in everything that we do. Then not to worry overmuch about what we do as we let you and life do with us what you will, and so become more fully ourselves and members of you. Amen.

3

His Temptation

Immediately after baptism there follows temptation. That is the inevitable sequence. Mark describes the essential nature of temptation thus:

> The Spirit immediately drove him out into the wilderness. And he was in the wilderness forty days, tempted by Satan; and he was with the wild beasts; and the angels ministered to him. (Mark 1:12–13)

After the initial exaltation of baptism when Christ knew fully who he was—the beloved son of his father— and experienced that deep sense of God's presence descending upon him, he was then driven by the Spirit and left alone in the wilderness. Nobody was there except wild beasts. There he had to decide alone whether he was now to act like himself—the Son of God—or whether he could settle for something a little less than that. Once he has made his decision, he again senses the presence of God's Spirit. The angels come and minister to him.

That sounds pretty familiar, doesn't it? Doesn't your own experience testify to the same essential characteristics of what temptation is? Whatever the particular

15

temptations may be, temptation itself is always the same. Once you have had a picture of yourself as you believe you truly are, and you have made up your mind on how you are going to spend the rest of your life, you go out with a real, deep sense of identity; but shortly thereafter you discover it doesn't quite work out that way.

You wonder if that picture you had of yourself was a false one. You find that you are not living the way you had made up your mind to live, in accordance with your nature, but in another way. The ideal "you" does not seem to have much relationship to the real "you." The real you does not measure up. You say, "I guess I misread myself." Or you say, "What's the use?" If you use religious language you might say, "God seems to have abandoned me." It can be very desolate. To say "I am not who I thought I was" can be—after you have known in the depth of your being who you were—a shattering experience. To have a sense of being abandoned by God—after you have genuinely sensed his presence—can be, in the true sense of the word, *dreadful*. It is an experience filled with dread; no one, no person, no God; only wilderness and wild beasts tearing you inside.

The temptation of Jesus is ours in part—the temptation not to ever become ourselves, the temptation to act contrary to our true nature, a willingness to become who we are not, the temptation to give up, to forget it, the temptation to no longer trust our own selves or God. When we give way to temptation, the ones we hurt most, of course, are ourselves. So it gets worse and worse, rather than better and better.

Call to mind one or two of the genuine temptations that you have been confronted with. Has not their essential nature always been this: that you are tempted to act contrary to yourself, tempted to act contrary to the

self you know you essentially are—and you betray yourself? The specific temptations can be anything under
the sun—adultery, anger, dishonesty, pride, self-righteousness, violence (violence of the spirit if not of the
flesh). But the essential quality of temptation is always
the same—you are not yourself, you deny your true self.
The temptation for Jesus was not to live in accordance
with his nature. For us it is exactly the same: the temptation not to live in accordance with what we know our
nature to be.

There is a similarity between his experience and
ours. But there is also a dissimilarity: he *always* lived in
accordance with his essential nature in obedience to his
father's will. The command of his father to obey him
was exactly the same as his obedience to him—
obedience to love. That is different from our existence.
He obeyed; we do not. Sometimes we do, but most
often we do not.

But has it not been true that on those occasions when
you have resisted temptation you have had a deep sense
of being confirmed in yourself? You know you are in
touch with the essential reality of your nature. When
you have really said "No," when you have deliberately
decided after a long tug of war inside to make that sac-
rificial choice willingly, no matter how painful it is,
have you not then felt more at home with yourself, at
home with life and the whole process of living? Have
you not felt glad to be alive? Life has affirmed you; you
were right and you have lived in accordance with your
nature. You affirm yourself. God affirms you. Angels
come and minister to you. God's presence strengthens
you.

It is a curious part of the mystery of human existence
that we do in fact have experiences like this. We do,
once in a while, resist temptation. We do, every so
often, become more and more ourselves; we are con-

firmed in what we know about ourselves; we know what we are talking about. We know "what's what" about us. We know this, and yet the curious fact is that we don't always act in accordance with what we know. We act exactly the opposite. When temptation comes, more often than not, we say "Yes" to it, and thus say "No" to ourselves and to God. That's strange! But that's the way it is.

If Jesus came to give us help, how do we get hold of that help? Let me try to answer with three brief suggestions. First, when you know who you are (or when you know you are in the process of touching yourself and that knowledge is growing, and you are in touch with an inner reality of that which is uniquely you, and you are honestly trying to live in accordance with that best inner self), as you go ahead in life you are led by the Spirit—indeed you may have a sense of being *driven* by the Spirit. When you have to make decisions in accordance with your nature, there is no alternative. That is the Spirit driving you.

Therefore *any* temptation may be all right. You do not have to agonize because you are tempted. That is what happens when you live in accordance with your nature and the Spirit calling you. Indeed, if you don't have any temptations, then it is time to worry. That is a sign that you are complacent, and complacency means self-righteousness and refusal to grow. To grow spiritually is to grow through temptations. You are led to them when you are in the Spirit most of all. So temptations that come within this framework are all right.

Secondly, when you are tempted, accept that nature of yours, that ideal nature and the real nature—the nature that you are and the nature that you hope to become, accepting it as the vision of yourself. Don't let that vision ever go. When you do, you are dead. Hold on to it. That is the essential you. Accept that, *and* accept the other you—your sins just as they are. Don't pretend they aren't there. Identify them. Accept them. That is part of the reality of who you are. The acceptance of them is part of the reality of who Christ is. To accept them, naming them specifically, is to confess them. Don't fight them. Confess them.

Only God can overcome sin. We cannot. If we think we can, we think we are God. That is the worst of all. That is why the moralistic man—the moral man who is proud of his goodness—is such an insufferable man. He pretends to be God, and he is set more against God than the immoral man.

Thus, the second suggestion is to accept ourselves as human beings, accept and hold our essential selves, confess ourselves; accept ourselves as part of humanity.

Finally, after accepting ourselves (or as we accept ourselves), accept Christ. I am not necessarily referring to a conversion experience, although that has a place in the emotional lives of some people and their decisions for Christ. I am referring to accepting Christ in another way—just going on, just starting again, just beginning once more to go about this business of living where you are in accordance with your nature as well as you can. You are just meant to be yourself. So get on with it! Start once more. Don't give up. Begin again. Accepting Christ means to accept his forgiveness. Then you can go on as forgiven sinners.

The only final sin is to give up. Christ says: Don't give up. Come unto me. You are forgiven. Accept that forgiveness. Then you will know what it is like to have angels come and minister to you.

Almighty God, whose blessed Son was led by the Spirit to be tempted by Satan: Come quickly to help us who are assaulted by many temptations; and, as you know the weaknesses of each of us, let each one find you mighty to save; through Jesus Christ your Son our Lord, who lives and reigns with you and the Holy Spirit, one God, now and forever. Amen.

4

His Teaching

After the angels had come to Jesus and ministered to him, he began his ministry in Galilee. He preached the Gospel, saying, "The time is fulfilled, and the kingdom of God is at hand; repent and believe in the gospel." He gathered his disciples around him and together they traveled through the villages and towns of Galilee. He began to teach what this Gospel meant. And as the people listened to him, saw him in action, they were, says St. Matthew, "all amazed" so that "they questioned among themselves, saying 'What is this? A new teaching!' With authority he commands even the unclean spirits, and they obey him. And at once his fame spread everywhere throughout all the surrounding region of Galilee."

Let us look more carefully at one of the stories that Jesus told:

> "Every one then who hears these words of mine and does them will be like a wise man who built his house upon the rock; and the rain fell, and the floods came, and the winds blew and beat upon that house, but it did not fall, because it

had been founded on the rock. And every one
who hears these words of mine and does not do
them will be like a foolish man who built his
house upon the sand; and the rain fell, and the
floods came, and the winds blew and beat
against that house, and it fell; and great was the
fall of it."

And when Jesus finished these sayings, the
crowds were astonished at his teaching, for he
taught them as one who had authority, and not
as their scribes. (Matthew 7:24–28)

What did Jesus teach? He taught that all human relationships depend, not only on external action, but on internal disposition. It is necessary, he said, not only to
act in a fair manner toward others, but to *be* fair; not
only to act in justice, but to *be* just; not only to do acts
of mercy, but to *be* merciful. It is not enough, he said,
to refrain from hostile acts toward one another. If a man
gives you a coat, give him two coats. If he wants you to
go with him for one mile on his journey, go an extra
mile. It is one thing, he said, never to commit adultery;
it is something else never to be lustful. You are meant,
he said, to be perfect, just as your heavenly father is
perfect. If you live in this kind of harmony with yourself
and your neighbor and your God, he concludes, then
your life will be like that of the man whose house was
built on a rock. When the rains fell and the floods came
and the winds blew, it did not fall because it was founded upon the rock. But if you hear these sayings of mine,
he said, and don't live them, you will be washed away
when the rains come. That, he said, is the Truth.

What do you think? The test that you apply to it is
yours. True, or false? On the basis of your own life and
the experiences you have had, does this seem true or
does it have a hollow ring? Have you, for example, ever
had someone in your life you just despised? He, or she,

was so awful that just to see that person made your blood boil; you crossed the street rather than have to say hello. When you saw him or her you had shocks of terror, disgust, or anger that shook you. You may have tried to do everything you could to get that person out of your life, to cut him off, to forget him. But he wouldn't go. And the terror, disgust, or anger just gnawed away inside, a cancer destroying you, making you someone you know you are not, worse than you are. Though you refrained from ever doing anything against that person, perhaps not even talking about him, you still had that gnawing away inside and you knew that if you were ever going to do anything about him, you had to do something with your own insides—and if you prayed, the only prayer that was an honest prayer was, "Give me a clean heart. Change my attitude toward that person. Do something that will make my inner disposition different when I think of him or her." It was a different disposition that was needed; and if, fortunately, a different spirit did come upon you, you found you had a different attitude; you began to behave differently; you may even have become reconciled to that person and he or she became a friend—maybe, in time, your closest friend.

You can test the truth of Jesus' sayings. It is not just external action, it is internal disposition, both together. Test it. What is the truth about yourself? As you are able to evaluate the truth about yourself, you can evaluate the truth about Jesus—not one or the other, but both together. Can you say, just on the basis of experiences that you have already had, "When I have the right spirit, *I'm* right. When I have the right spirit, I try automatically to do the right thing. It is a spontaneous thing, not calculating. When I am in touch with myself and in harmony with myself, with my own interior life, I tend to be more in harmony with my neighbors and those around me. I even sense, sometimes, that when I have that touch, I am in harmony with God. Everything seems to be more of a piece in my life, and I am more able to take the disjointed parts of it that don't fit in very easily. The movement of my life seems to be toward a purpose or a goal which draws me, to which I know I belong; once attained, I will move on to another goal, another purpose. But in that process I have a deep sense that I belong to life, I am living it, I am being carried by it."

If that—or something like it—is a truth that you can affirm about yourself, then you can more readily understand Christ when he says, "I am the Truth." He is whole. The outward action and the inner spirit correspond. The truth, the only truth, is that interior spirit which is in touch with the reality of life, the ultimate reality of life, when you are able to be yourself with absolute integrity. You can act with love and integrity even against the grain of life. You are then in touch with the spirit which carries all cross grains. When you are in that spirit you can say, "I am really myself. That is the truth. I am that truth." That spirit is Christ the Truth.

How do you know that? There is no way except by living it. You know it by your life, by your love, by your own integrity, by the measure to which you are already an authentic person. You know it by your spirit. You know it as you *do* it. You know it as you *are* it. Ultimate truth is always *lived* truth. Ultimate truth about the mystery of existence is apprehended in the only way by which persons are apprehended—that is, by trusting and loving. It's you and your person, it's your neighbor and his or her person, and the person, Jesus Christ, all mixed together.

There is an old saying (by Plotinus), "By love God is gotten and holden; by thought never." Just as you never get hold of God by thinking about him, only by loving him, you can never get to know a person just by thinking about him. You know him only, finally, as you love him.

So the conclusion of the matter is this: the only way to understand the teachings of Jesus is to come to *him*. Once you have thought about his teachings, examined them, looked at them, tried to live them, to be perfect as your father is perfect, and faced up to the truth about yourself—your failure to live them, your failure to live them combined always with your longing to live them (it's the longing and the failing together)—once you have tried to live his teachings, then you are ready to come to him. It is not his teachings we long for, it is him. We need *him*, not information about him, not even information about how we should live. We know, pretty much, how to live.

We hear his invitation: "Come unto me. I will refresh you. Take my yoke upon you. Learn from me. I am gentle and lowly in heart. You will find rest for your souls. For my yoke is easy and my burden is light."

We learn from him. So let us come to him. Trust him; he will teach you of himself. He knows us infinitely better than we know ourselves. As we come increasingly to know him, we shall become ourselves more perfect as our father in heaven is perfect, and therefore more freely ourselves.

So come. Take, eat, drink. You will find rest.

That is the way to begin again to have a new spirit within you, a new disposition, a new attitude toward life, so you can take anything that comes. That is the way to a new, *true* you. When the rain falls, and the floods come, and the winds blow and beat upon you, you will not fall because you are founded upon the rock—the eternal truth of Christ and of yourself. So come.

O Lord Jesus—
  You were faithful to your nature,
    Help us to be faithful to ours.
  You were obedient to your Father's command
    to love in your life;
    Help us obey your commands
    to love in your life;
  You were faithful to your nature,
    We have.

  So we confess our sins to you,
    and thank you for taking them away.
  When next temptation comes,
    you take our place,
    you conquer it.

  You say No for us,
    so we may say Yes to ourselves.
  And so go on in newness of life
    praising you for saving us.

O Lord Jesus Christ,

  When we are in touch with the truth about ourselves,
  we are in touch with you.

  So we thank you for having showed us some truth
  about ourselves, and so about you.

  We come to you now because you call us,
  because you have already come to us.

  As we respond to the truths we know,
  so we shall come at last to know you who art the
    truth.

  In the meantime, help us to live and love you,
  our neighbors, and ourselves.

                              Amen.

5

His Ministry

St. Mark records these incidents from the ministry of Jesus:

> And Jesus went on with his disciples, to the villages of Caesarea Philippi; and on the way he asked his disciples, "Who do men say that I am?" And they told him, "John the Baptist; and others say, Elijah; and others one of the prophets." And he asked them, "But who do you say that I am?" Peter answered him, "You are the Christ." And he charged them to tell no one about him.
>
> And he began to teach them that the Son of man must suffer many things, and be rejected by the elders and the chief priests and the scribes, and be killed, and after three days rise again. And he said this plainly. And Peter took him, and began to rebuke him. But turning and seeing his disciples, he rebuked Peter, and said, "Get behind me, Satan! For you are not on the side of God, but of men."
>
> And he called to him the multitude with his disciples, and said to them, "If any man would come after me, let him deny himself and take

up his cross and follow me. For whoever would save his life will lose it; and whoever loses his life for my sake and the gospel's will save it. For what does it profit a man, to gain the whole world and forfeit his life? For what can a man give in return for his life? For whoever is ashamed of me and of my words in this adulterous and sinful generation, of him will the Son of man also be ashamed, when he comes in the glory of his Father with the holy angels."

And he said to them, "Truly, I say to you, there are some standing here who will not taste death before they see the kingdom of God come with power."

And after six days Jesus took with him Peter and James and John, and led them up a high mountain apart by themselves; and he was transfigured before them, and his garments became glistening, intensely white, as no fuller on earth could bleach them. And there appeared to them Elijah with Moses; and they were talking to Jesus. And Peter said to Jesus, "Master, it is well that we are here; let us make three booths, one for you and one for Moses and one for Elijah." For he did not know what to say, for they were exceedingly afraid. And a cloud overshadowed them, and a voice came out of the cloud, "This is my beloved Son; listen to him." And suddenly looking around they no longer saw any one with them but Jesus only. (Mark 8:27–9:8)

Jesus' ministry did not last very long—at the most three years, possibly only one year. Nor did it cover very much ground. Galilee was smaller than Vermont, made up primarily of small towns and villages. Jesus spent most of his time out there in the countryside; only toward the end of his life did he go into the capital city to preach. And he did not accomplish very much in his ministry. He did some preaching and teaching, healed some people who were sick, influenced some friends who traveled with him—but not very decisively because when he died they disbanded whatever little organization they had.

The significance of his ministry is not so much in his *performance* as in his *presence*. Rather, his presence and his performance were identical. What he said and did expressed who he was. There was a complete identity between his words, his actions, and himself. He was authentic. He "flowed" when he spoke and when he acted. There was no conflict between his performance and his presence. He lived God's will in all that he said and all that he did every moment and through all the circumstances of his life. *That* was his ministry.

His ministry was his service to mankind by showing forth in a wholly consistent life that love is more powerful than anything set against it, even death. So his ministry—to serve people, to bring them life—was accomplished by his obeying God. In him the *command* to love and his *obedience* to love were exactly the same. He was fully who he was meant to be. His life was all of a piece, wholly and freely living himself. *That* was his ministry.

The Bible passage above marks a decisive change in that public ministry. After it was clear to Jesus that his disciples had not come to any certain understanding of who he was, or what it meant to be Christ, there followed the transfiguration in which Jesus' closest friends, Peter, James and John, received the same confirmation that Jesus had received at his baptism when they heard the words, "This is my beloved son; listen to him." Once that had been proclaimed so that they knew it as well as Jesus, the ministry took a decisive turn. From this time forward the somewhat leisurely journeying from village to village and town to town ends. Preparation begins next for that move toward Jerusalem. The hitherto uneasiness between the religious authorities and Jesus sharpens now into a dispute. The forces that are arrayed in the struggle begin to tighten and converge on that journey toward Jerusalem as the little band prepares to enter the conflict. The public ministry is almost at an end.

What can we say about this ministry and its implications for us in our ministry? As we have observed, the story of Jesus Christ is in some measure our story as well. As we learn to read his story, we are helped to read the story of our own lives. Contrariwise, as we read our story, we are helped to read his. It is all for one purpose: that the story of our lives which we write might become increasingly consistent with his; that we may in fact become ourselves—the selves that God had in mind for us from before the creation of the world—so that we might increasingly become those unique persons we are.

Let me suggest three characteristics of his ministry. First, in his public ministry, Jesus moved very naturally among the people, taking them as they were, knowing just what he had to do. He accepted very naturally all the human circumstances, the different kinds of people, and the ordinary events. The first miracle he performed was at a wedding reception. Throughout his ministry he healed people who were sick in mind or body. He comforted a mother at the funeral of her only son by bringing him back to life. He fed the multitudes when they were hungry. When his disciples were frightened by a storm at sea, he calmed the waves. He lifted up little children and said, "if you want to enter God's Kingdom, you are going to have to trust the way these little children trust." He talked with prostitutes, tax collectors, poor people, outcasts. He seemed more at

home with those in the lower classes than those in the
upper classes. He lived day and night during those
years of public ministry with twelve people whom he
had selected, and in particular, those closest three
friends. He went, in a word, since his ministry was to
all mankind, to all sorts and conditions of men. He did
this because he simply had to do what he had to do. He
did what he had to do.

Our ministry is no more than just that—no more, no
less than just going about our lives doing what we have
to do. It is getting up in the morning and sometimes
just hanging on through the day. There are days when
we have to settle for just being able to hang on—to go
about our business, do our job, meet our obligations,
carry out whatever word we have given to people even
if it is not to our own benefit; to try to be decent
members of our families and of our society, to be faithful wherever the circumstances of life have brought us.
We bring service to others by being loyal to our best
selves, to those we are bound to and to those who stand
beyond us and are different from us. One of the characteristics of the Church is that we assume some responsibility of service to those who do not belong to us, but
who belong to Christ just as much as we do. Ministry is
going about our day-to-day work.

Secondly, Christ not only *went out* to people, he also
withdrew from them. He was a private person. He withdrew from constantly going about his business and
being with the crowds at all times. Sometimes he withdrew with his disciples, sometimes with his particular
friends, often by himself. He prayed. He prayed not
only in public, but in private. He probably prayed by not
doing much except being quiet, reflecting. He prayed to
his father in secret. There he wrestled with his mission.
He wrestled with the question of who he was and how
he was to carry out his ministry, what it meant, what

his father's will was, how he could make sense of what he was called to do. It was out of that inner personal relationship with God that there developed his conviction about the meaning of his life and how he could best express it. There inwardly, as we say, it came to him what he was to do.

The obvious question then is, who do you pay attention to when you are by yourself? Do you talk to anybody? Do you realize that there is an interior self you can talk with, where you can have the most intimate personal conversations with God? You need not only psychologically withdraw from time to time from the busy-ness of life and have a vacation (although that's important), but you need to withdraw from the pressures of life that are *external* in order that you may listen to the pressures of life that are *internal*. It is through those inner pressures where God is speaking, where you sense that you are being called freely to become yourself—to be yourself with integrity. What should you do then? That is where the conversations take place to get a renewed sense of direction for your life and to discover what you should do. The practice of the presence of God—the sense of his immediacy and the waiting upon him, heeding, listening, attending—is what the practice of prayer is. When you are alone, he is as near to you as you are to yourself. To pray to him is really no more than to look at him and let him look at you and in that light look at yourself. To cultivate the art of solitude seems to be one of the requirements if we are to live as free, whole people carrying out any ministry to anyone else. There in the quiet of our inner life we sense that spirit which is uniquely ours, where we are most in touch with ourselves.

The third and final characteristic is this: in the person of Jesus, God was present with power. As men and women listened to him and saw what he did, they said to one another, "This man speaks with an authority we have never heard before. He knows what he is talking about. We have never heard anybody like him. We marvel! We are astonished!" When they trusted him, they discovered they no longer were afraid. They said, "We trust you, Jesus. You are able to take our lives and help us be ourselves."

Because he was himself, he ministered to the people. His ministry was his presence.

What do you bring to minister to other people? You bring your presence. That is all you can bring. That is a great deal because no one else can bring it. You are uniquely yourself. And the more you bring freely of your own inner, authentic life in response to the person you believe yourself to be, the greater power you bring to people. The more what you say and what you do jibes with who you are, the more power will be given. No consistency, no power; no wholeness, no power.

To give yourself, you need to be in possession of yourself. You cannot give away what you do not have. To possess yourself is to be at one with yourself. Then you do not have to worry about what you will be doing—all you have to do is be yourself and you will know what to do.

How do you do that? As you hold yourself accountable to the best that you know of yourself, you hold yourself accountable to Christ. As you try to obey him, you minister to those around you. For then you give not just yourself, but you give them *him*. That is God's power. That reassures people and it helps them to live their lives more strongly because of you and your presence and the way you deal with your life.

That is God's power, and the way to get it is to give it. That is Christ's gift of his ministry to your ministry. That is the gift of Christ.

To be yourself, then, is in a curious, mysterious way

to become *him*. That is the miracle of Christ's life and ministry as it is ours.

> It is our business, O Lord, to give as much of ourselves as we know to as much of you as we know; help us, therefore, to know ourselves more and more so that we may come to know you more and more, and as we come to know you, come then to love you more and more, and so love ourselves and our neighbors as ourselves, through Jesus Christ our Lord. Amen.

6

His Journey Toward Jerusalem

We mentioned earlier that the ministry of Jesus was carried out for the most part in the villages and towns of Galilee and that it underwent a decisive turning point after the events of Caesarea Philippi and the transfiguration. He began then to "turn his face toward Jerusalem." St. Mark writes thus of that journey undertaken after Jesus had made the decision to bring his public ministry to a close, to go up to Jerusalem and there engage the powers of the established religion and of the state:

> And they were on the road, going up to Jerusalem, and Jesus was walking ahead of them; and they were amazed, and those who followed were afraid. And taking the twelve again, he began to tell them what was to happen to him, saying, "Behold, we are going up to Jerusalem; and the Son of man will be delivered to the chief priests and the scribes, and they will condemn him to death, and deliver him to the Gentiles; and they will mock him, and spit upon

him, and scourge him, and kill him; and after
three days he will rise." (Mark 10:32–34)

The first point that can be made about this journey is
that now the die is cast. The decision is made. The
months of preparation in the public ministry and the
years in his hidden life have now come to an end. He
has made the decision now to present his message. His
message is himself; he will present himself in the capital city. That message is: God's Kingdom is here. The
reality of God is already present. Jesus is going to con-
front the authorities with the authority of God in person. He is going to present the rule of God as the only
rule that ever lasts. That rule is the rule of love in personal relationships and justice in social relationships.
The purpose of the journey is to let those who are
threatened by such a message and by such a person
come to grips with him face to face. How will the religious and civil authorities who already possess religious and civil power respond to the reality of God?

If you are afraid of love, what do you do when someone comes into your life loving you? When you have
been unable to love no matter how much you have
wanted to, what happens when you discover that there
is a person who does indeed love you? If you do not like
equal justice for everyone but instead want a special
position of privilege for yourself, how do you act when
you discover that that day is going? What do you do in
response to the forces which hasten or to the person
who hastens the coming of that day when your privilege is no more and justice reigns freely for all men?
How do you respond to that kind of presence among
you?

The purpose of Jesus' journey toward Jerusalem was
to find this out. What happens when love confronts the

unlovable and justice faces prejudice? We are going to find out as his story unfolds.

The second thing that can be said about Jesus' journey is that the disciples tagged along. They did not lead the way; they followed. They were bewildered, frightened, uncertain about what was to take place, knowing something terribly important was going to happen to their leader, but baffled as to what that might be. They seemed totally unable to comprehend what was going on no matter how often Jesus tried to explain it to them. The Bible passage above tells of the third time that Jesus took the disciples away from the crowds and instructed them so that they might know what to expect. He said, "We are going up to Jerusalem and I am going to be delivered to the chief priests and scribes. They are going to condemn me to death, they will put me in the hands of the Roman authorities. They will mock, spit, scourge, kill me; and after three days I will rise."

They just could not grasp it. All during the next week, they could not understand. They never understood until *afterwards*. The moment that Jesus finished telling them what was going to happen, two of his favorite disciples said, "Will you put us on the right hand and on the left hand in glory right away?" How pained he must have been by such a question. Though they stayed with him, still tagging along during those days that followed, when he was finally put to death, they fled. They were not unlike most of us. We tag along. We are pretty baffled by life—fearful sometimes, sometimes terrified of the things that might happen, unaware of what to expect fully.

Jesus is ahead of us. We follow at a distance, not quite understanding. We usually do not understand until afterwards. It is after the event that the illumination comes and we are struck by what we see. We keep on tagging along. And that, strangely enough, is enough.

The third thing that can be said is that Jesus never spoke about his death without speaking about his resurrection. "I will be put to death, and I will rise." Five times he makes reference to his death *and* resurrection—never to his death alone. Indeed he came finally to say, "I am the resurrection."

The disciples could not believe that this was at all possible. They could not believe this until the resurrection had taken place. It was then that they saw that the defeat of death was in fact a victory, that fear was in fact overcome by love, that all human weakness is—in God—turned into power. It was then, afterwards, that they began to live. *He* was raised and so *they* were raised. When they lived that kind of a positive, confident, powerful life they showed *him* as raised. The disciples in a curious way became *him*. That spirit has helped to make later Christians live with some kind of an affirmative attitude toward life no matter what it brings.

They finally understood when an event—the resurrection—took place that was beyond human comprehension. It came finally to those who trusted him.

Can we now translate that journey to Jerusalem into our own journeys—the journeys of our own lives? We know on the basis of our own experiences that there are certain times in life when we have to make fundamental decisions. Once we have made them, we have to proceed to live with them and be responsible for them. There are certain times in life when we can't fake it anymore. There are certain times in life when position, privilege or accomplishments mean nothing. The nettle is there and it has to be seized.

Life is a series of decisions that we make in response to certain kinds of pressures. What do you do when death strikes someone you love? What happens when your resources suddenly disappear? What happens when you know you are found out? When the utter reality of life—and death—descends?

Can you seize the nettle and move into it, make a decision and live with it? You know already that when you have done that, you've come out on the other side on a higher plateau. The indecision and the wavering are gone because you have faced reality and moved right into it, no matter how painful it may be. You have grasped it. In the grasping of that decision, your own integrity and selfhood are restored and you become more of a person than you were before.

That is to go up to Jerusalem. Once you start going, you never know what will happen, except that life won't turn out the way you think it is going to. Life, someone has said, is what happens to you when you're making other decisions. One thing you can count on is that if you do act in this fashion and have made these decisions, as you trust the decision and trust life, you discover that it begins to carry you. You don't have to do it by yourself; life helps you do it if you trust it, if you move into it—not if you give up, not if you trust your fears, not if you become afraid, not if you withdraw and cut off, and cut off, and cut off. You are cutting yourself off. But if you sometimes just tag along, you discover that you are carried. You are carried and life turns out, when you trust it, to be better than you expected no matter what happens. Life is better. And there is more richness in store for you.

To trust life is to trust death and resurrection together. It is to trust the process of not getting your own way because you want to express some kind of love in your life. It is to be willing not to try to get everything for yourself, because in some measure you want to stand for justice for others, even though it may be to your disadvantage to do so. As you make this kind of decision—the decision of trust—those decisions reflect more and more of your true nature. You become more than you were.

Resurrection and death are together: that, in a word, is to trust Jesus. You can use another word if you are easier with it—integrity, life, love, conviction, justice. But the Christian faith says all that is to trust Jesus; it just rises out of life. Those experiences have to have a name, and what our trust is in, is in the name because there must be a name to describe the reality we have already experienced. You don't have to understand everything about him or about life. Who does? To trust him is simply to follow him. If you tag along, going through those experiences of life and death and resurrection, you can't help but come to know him and try to follow him; so when the pressures of life force you to make a decision, you do so in accordance with his story and your own. You put them together. It is a great story.

And it's done. That's the miracle of it. It is not something that might happen only to some saints—it happens to ordinary people. It happens to a man who is stricken with a heart attack. He lies in his bed and says, "I'm ready for anything." That is some story! It is not only his story, it is Christ's story. A woman is told she has cancer and she says, "My life is going to move on now around a brand new experience. I'm looking forward to this." That is some story!

Those are real life stories. Those are stories of Jesus' life, death, resurrection. True life stories—his journey to Jerusalem, our journey to Jerusalem, through the streets and beyond—an eternal journey we take together.

> *You came not to be ministered unto*
> *but to minister.*

Your ministry was your presence
and it still is.
So we thank you for your presence
among us and within us.
Since we are most ourselves
when we are most attentive to you
and obey you,
Help us go about our daily business
with your spirit
And to know that when we pray,
it is you praying within us.
So may we carry out our ministry
and yours.

Lord Jesus,

> *Leader in our journeys, King of life*
> *and death, and resurrection,*
> *creator of light and darkness,*
> *revealer of mystery and eternity,*

> *Don't get too far ahead of us.*
> *But don't let us rest or go back either.*

> *You have called us to life.*
> *Keep us tagging along.*

> *And when the crises come, help us*
> *to be true to ourselves, true to you,*
> *and so more ourselves transformed by you*
> *into you so that we may bring life.*

> *And so on our journey go on our way*
> *rejoicing in you and with those*
> *whom you have given to us—*
> *our companions along the way.*
>   *Amen.*

7

His Worship

The first thing Jesus did when he had chosen his disciples was to go with them on the Sabbath day into the synagogue and share in the worship of his people. It was clear that he identified himself completely with his people and with their worship. To be sure, he had disputes with the religious leaders—including in his last days on earth a fatal dispute—but nowhere did he turn against the religion of his fathers. St. Mark records it:

> And they went into Capernaum; and immediately on the sabbath he entered the synagogue and taught. And they were astonished at his teaching, for he taught them as one who had authority, and not as the scribes. And immediately there was in their synagogue a man with an unclean spirit; and he cried out, "What have you to do with us, Jesus of Nazareth? Have you come to destroy us? I know who you are, the Holy One of God." But Jesus rebuked him, saying, "Be silent, and come out of him!" And the unclean spirit, convulsing him and crying with a loud voice, came out of him.
>
> And they were all amazed, so that they ques-

> tioned among themselves, saying, "What is this? A new teaching! With authority he commands even the unclean spirits, and they obey him." And at once his fame spread everywhere throughout all the surrounding region of Galilee. (Mark 1:21–28)

He was a member in good standing of those who belonged to the Covenant of Sinai established by God with his forebears, Abraham, Isaac, and Jacob. He criticized the institutional forms, lifted the sights of people above the legalism of his day, but he did not come, he said, to destroy the Law and the Prophets, but to fulfill them. When he worshipped, he worshipped in the synagogue. Trained in his parents' religion from childhood, it provided in all probability the substance as well as the form of his education. He worshipped with the people of the God of Israel. He did not repudiate the worship of his people; he came to renew it.

He began his ministry with worship through the Old Covenant. And when he ended it, he established the New Covenant, again an act of worship:

> And as they were eating, he took bread, and blessed, and broke it, and gave it to them, and said, "Take; this is my body." And he took a cup, and when he had given thanks he gave it to them, and they all drank of it. And he said to them, "This is my blood of the covenant, which is poured out for many. Truly, I say to you, I shall not drink again of the fruit of the vine until that day when I drink it new in the kingdom of God."
>
> And when they had sung a hymn, they went out to the Mount of Olives. (Mark 14:22–26)

"Now," he says, on the night in which he was betrayed, "here is the New Covenant: my body and blood,

my life and my spirit; *I* am the new Covenant; in me
there is now a new relationship between you and God;
henceforth he sees you through my eyes; and you see
him through mine. In me there is now a new relationship of the father to his children. So, take this bread,
blessed, broken; this is my body. And take this cup,
drink of it; this is my blood of the Covenant which is
poured out for many."

This has been called the Last Supper. It is really the
First Supper. The Last Supper was the first in a series
of suppers that have been going on for two thousand
years in every tongue and in every land, suppers where
all sorts and conditions of men and women and
children—high and low, rich and poor, kings and
beggars—have gathered together to take bread, to eat it,
to bless the cup and drink it, to declare once again that
now in Christ they have a new relationship to God; they
are his children, members of Christ's body and inher-
itors of his Kingdom.

Whatever the variety of forms by which this service is
celebrated, they all strike this common note: Jesus
Christ is here. He is here in this community of people.
He is here in the worshipping community. He is here,
an inner spiritual presence in an outward form. How do
we get this sense of his presence?

For most Christian people today the one conscious,
corporate activity in which they take part is the one
hour weekly service of worship. It should, therefore, be
their "spiritual" high point of the week in the sense that
they are in this gathering reminded once again of who
they are as God's children; they are renewed both by
the preaching of the Word "to their condition" and by
their eucharistic offering; they are renewed in the Spirit
and so strengthened for their daily life in the world
where God has placed them.

If the worship is "in spirit and in truth," then there is

vitality. If there is dis-spiritedness or falsity, then there is no worship. It is as simple—and aweful—as that.

It means we are meant to bring our authentic selves to worship—no pretend selves, show selves, phony selves. But if we do bring these false selves, it is to rid ourselves of them—by asking forgiveness as we confess our sins, to lay before God where "the truth is not in us," and expectantly in hope to have, by faith, a new, open, clean, vigorous life.

And when the minister brings the same kind of authenticity in his person and preaches in the same spirit, then spirit speaks to spirit and the Word of God for each person is heard. The Word empowers. But it empowers only those who try to live by its spirit. Only those who have ears to hear can hear.

So worship in one form or another, identity with the people of God, has always been the central, essential part of the Christian life. Every act of worship is an act whereby we set forth once again what the New Covenant means, what the new relationship with God is.

It is a very simple act—an act that we do together. There are three steps to it. The first is that it is an act of *remembrance.* The question is, how *do you* remember him? Each of us probably remembers him somewhat differently. If you are a young person, you think of him differently than you do if you are an adult. If you are an adult, you can remember how you thought of him as a young person, and how you think of him now.

You think of him in any number of different ways. You may remember him and think of him primarily as someone whose presence is comforting, reassuring and strengthening. You know that your ultimate security is in him. Or, you may think of him rather uneasily with a conscience that is not quite at ease with itself, and you are sometimes a little sorry that you remember him. He does not ever let you get away with being content with your life. He keeps goading you, pulling you, tugging you, judging you. Or maybe you remember him as one who above all else has forgiven you, and who has therefore strengthened you and encouraged you and said, "O.K., you are forgiven. Now get up on your feet and act like an adult. No more indulging yourself in guilt feelings or the luxury of melancholia or self-pity. Get up!"

Remember him any way you want to, any way that is most helpful. That undoubtedly is part of what went on that first night when the disciples were engaged in this act that they could never understand fully and did not understand until after his resurrection. But they did remember him and they did think of him as he gave this astounding news that here he was. What they brought to mind were their memories of what he had done for them in the boat in the storm, and the way he had fed the multitudes when they were hungry, and how he had healed the sick, and raised the young man from the dead. They remembered him even though they could not fully understand the mystery of what was going on that night. Even though we cannot fully understand how he is present with us, we remember him. We do so especially as we remember those who have been God-bearers to us.

It is an act of *remembrance*. It is also an act of *thanksgiving*. In that first service, it was the Passover season and the service at the table began with the taking of bread by the head of the household and blessing God, thanking God for it. "Blessed be thou, O Lord, who givest food to the hungry." God is the one who is blessed; it is not the bread. So if you are bothered sometimes by what appears to be the manipulation of bread, remember that it is not the bread, but it is God who is blessed by the breaking of bread and by the remembrance of Jesus. "Feed on him in your heart with *thanksgiving.*"

On that first night the disciples, as Jesus did, gave thanks to God for all the gifts of life and, since it was the Passover season, in particular for his having delivered them from slavery in Egypt into freedom in the land of promise. How did the disciples remember *him?*

Remember *him*. His presence and his performance were one. His teaching was himself. Not new law but a new spirit. Not to *act* fairly so much as to *be* fair. To *be* just, to *be* merciful.

Think of the person who drives us up a wall. We need a new spirit, a new attitude. "When I have the right spirit, *I'm* right." To come to understand his teachings is to come to *him*. We long for him. *I* am the truth.

It is an act, finally, of *hope* and *expectancy*. We do not know now precisely how we shall see him, in what form "face to face" means; but by faith we are confident that we shall see *him*. The presence is what counts—not the appearance.

And in the same way in our more immediate lives, with the pressing concerns and problems that we present to him with his own self-offering, we do not *know* how things are going to work out, but we can be certain that so long as we work them out with *him* in his spirit—then they will work out better than "we can either hope or pray for."

So we can go on with buoyancy, with confidence, with infinite hope. We then know that all things do indeed work together for good as we love God. Our worship is our expression of our love. So it is in remembering Christ, thanking him, expecting him. It is remembering people loved and loving, thanking them, expecting to be one with them "in spirit and in truth"—forever.

>Almighty God, our heavenly father,

>when we gather together in the presence of one another in your name, let us always have a sense of your presence;

>when we meet one another, may we be alert to meet you;

>when we speak and when we listen to one another, may we be alert to hear your voice;

>and as we trust and love one another, let it be our trusting and loving you.

>This we pray we may do when we are gathered together in the presence of your Son, Jesus Christ our Lord. Amen.

8

His Prayer

And when they had sung a hymn," Mark says in describing the conclusion of the Last Supper, "they went out to the Mount of Olives."

Jesus and his disciples had completed their meal together. They had completed their worship together. They had sung a hymn together. Together they went out to the Mount of Olives. Then things began to break up. The disciples began to break up. Judas, first of all, had already gone to meet the religious authorities so that they might alert the state authorities. The chain of events leading to betrayal was under way. Then Jesus left the body of disciples and took with him his closest friends—Peter, James and John—and asked them to wait for him while he went yet further away to pray. When he prayed he had to be alone. We all do. Worship is corporate and public. Prayer is personal and private.

His prayer—and it is this with which we are concerned in this chapter—was a most human one: "I do not want to die. I want to live." But it was also the prayer of a loving son to a loving father: "What I want most of all is what you want. And I will do what you want." When after some time he came back and found his friends sleeping, he said, "Couldn't you even keep awake for one hour?" He did this twice more. Finally, the third time when he found them sleeping, he said, "All right, the time is come. The Son of Man is about to be betrayed into the hands of sinners. Get up. Let us go on. See, my betrayer is here."

Well, that is all very human, isn't it? Just like us. Just like our experiences. We are in trouble, deep trouble, with deep anxiety and fears about something. We want above all in such a time of crisis to have some friends around us who understand—friends who care for us. And they do care. Sometimes they are a great help. When we have gone through some traumatic experience, like losing someone we love or being betrayed, we are helped immeasurably just by talking it over with a friend. Just to be able to talk to friends about what is on our minds is an indispensable help, and sometimes that is all we need. But not always. Friends don't always produce. They don't always stick with us. During the long night watches they sometimes fall asleep. They don't always stay with us for the long haul. There are other things to do. Once the immediate crisis has been met, they sometimes drop out. And it is, of course, not simply "they" we are talking about, because "we" are the "they" when we are turned to by friends who come to us for help and we turn out to be no more satisfactory. We more easily call short term on friends in hospitals than long term on friends in nursing homes.

It has been said that this prayer of Jesus is the mark above all other marks of his humanity. He had now his life's work to accomplish. He needed the support of his friends, and he asked for it. They did what they could, but it was not enough. So finally he had to make the decision about what to do all by himself, alone—alone, that is, with his father. That is his prayer. It is the final mark of the highest humanity. To be human is to pray. It is to have friends and it is also to pray alone.

When Jesus found himself all alone, it was no more than what happens to us when we find ourselves all alone. Even if friends do not go to sleep, when we are faced with certain fundamental decisions in life we have to make them all alone. Nobody else can make them for us.

To belong to humanity means to belong to one another. We need one another, and yet others cannot meet our deepest needs because we have to make those deepest, individual decisions, those critical ones, all by ourselves. Decisions like . . . what is the action I must take to make my life count? Nobody else can tell us that. Decisions like . . . what do I do when things go wrong and there is no one I can turn to? What happens when I discover that I am all alone and the road is always uphill?

The experience of Jesus teaches us that we can do anything we want to do—provided it is right. If it is not right, it won't get us anywhere—and it won't get anybody else anywhere. A wrong action never leads to a right result. In biblical language, if our action is not in accord with God's will it won't work. In the long run it won't work. That is why Jesus and we pray, "What do you want? What you want is what I want." What he wants is always what we know is right.

Most of the time we know what is right. We may not do it, but we know it. Not always, though, because sometimes we just do not know what is right. The crisscrossing of loyalties is too great. Try as we will, we cannot seem to get a clear picture. We pray, and we don't get an answer. What is the answer?

The only answer to unanswered prayer seems to be more prayer. By that I do not mean more asking. God already knows all about that. I mean more "pressing into God," more waiting upon him, more paying attention to him, more simply holding yourself before him, more being "intent" toward him, more doing nothing, just being, being centered in him, more being aware of him, sensitive to him, just knowing you are in him and expecting, anticipating him.

When you are going through an experience like this, you are on the verge of a significant breakthrough in your relationship to God. He has brought you to this point through all your growing-up experiences in prayer in order that you may take the next step into mature Christian prayer. When there is no answer to your question to God—"What do you want?"—only silence, in that silence he is turning the question around and asking you, "What do *you* want? What do you in Christ want? You are a grown-up mature partner with me now. In Christ you are my friend. What now in this experience do you want to do for your love of me? Well, do it. Whatever you want to do for Christ's sake, do it. What *you* want to do in Christ is what I want."

So you decide. You make up your mind. How else can Christ deal with the matter, except to let you decide? You are one in him.

It is this which is Christian freedom wherein we are set free to live truly as children of God. So you decide. Offer the decision to God. And to go on freely to live is to be freely yourself, your own unique self—in Christ. And it is also how Christ is freely himself in you.

There is a saying by a medieval mystic—Meister Eckhardt—which seems appropriate: "The eye with which you see God is the eye with which God sees you." The eye is Christ. Look at God through Christ's eye—through his prayer, "not my will, but yours be done." This is the eye through which God sees you. The eye is one and in Christ you and God are one. So go live in him as he lives in you. Get on with living.

That is what Christ did when he came back the third time to his disciples and said, "All right, that is enough. The hour has come. Let us be going." He put his whole life into God's hands. And the only way he could do it was to put his life into the hands of the religious and state authorities. He put his destiny into their hands— but into their hands *under God's hands*. Our destinies always rest in the hands of others; but as long as they are *under God,* and we are the ones who put them there, his will destined for us (his design for us) is always carried out. It is not so much the content of our decisions which is significant as it is the context within which those decisions are made. The context is God's will and our will, both expressed through Christ. He is the eye through which we and God see each other and live and act together.

Jesus' prayer was a mark of his humanity. *Our* prayer is a mark of our divinity. His humanity and divinity, our divinity and humanity—together we are his body. And that body acts through us in our world. "What do you in your life want to do for your love of God?" Well, do it. Offer it to God. And get on with life.

> "The eye with which we see God is the eye with which God sees us." Therefore, Almighty God, help us to look at you through the eye of Christ. If we are uncertain of that eye, let us look at you through the eye of truth. And if we are uncertain of truth, let us look at you through our own hearts. Keep, therefore, those hearts clean, give them integrity, remove self-will, take away our fears, give us confidence in thee. Then

do you look upon us through the eye of your truth, as we have known the truth, and through the right as you give us to understand the right—so that all men in their common humanity may bear the marks of their divinity as they pray to do your will this night and always. Amen.

9

His Religious Trial

There are two trials. The first is before the religious authorities. The second is before the political authorities.

Here is Mark's description of the first trial:

> And they led Jesus to the high priest; and all the chief priests and the elders and the scribes were assembled. And Peter had followed him at a distance, right into the courtyard of the high priest; and he was sitting with the guards, and warming himself at the fire. Now the chief priests and the whole council sought testimony against Jesus to put him to death; but they found none. For many bore false witness against him, and their witness did not agree. And some stood up and bore false witness against him, saying, "We heard him say, 'I will destroy this temple that is made with hands, and in three days I will build another, not made with hands.'" Yet not even so did their testimony agree. And the high priest stood up in the midst, and asked Jesus, "Have you no answer to make? What is it that these men testify against you?" But he was silent and made no answer.

Again the high priest asked him, "Are you the
Christ, the Son of the Blessed?" And Jesus said,
"I am; and you will see the Son of man sitting
at the right hand of Power, and coming with the
clouds of heaven." And the high priest tore his
mantle, and said, "Why do we still need witnesses? You have heard his blasphemy. What is
your decision?" And they all condemned him as
deserving death. And some began to spit on
him, and to cover his face, and to strike him,
saying to him, "Prophesy!" And the guards received him with blows. (Mark 14:53–65)

Some historians question whether this was an official
meeting of the official body of the seventy-one members
of the Sanhedrin. That body was the supreme legisla-
tive authority determining the practices and the rules of
the Jewish faith, responsible for the administering of
the religious life of the Jews, distinct from the political
life of the Jews. It was controlled by Rome and its governor, Pontius Pilate. It is possible that this secret mid-
night meeting was a gathering, not of the whole Sanhedrin, but of a carefully selected number of top leaders;
and the hearing, not an official hearing, but more the
kind that is conducted by the Gestapo or the Mafia or
the Ku Klux Klan.

In any case, there is Jesus before Caiaphas, the high
priest, and his officials. In reality it was just the other
way around: the leaders of the establishment before
Jesus. The witnesses could not agree about the charges
against Jesus, so Caiaphas himself asked, "Well, are
you the Christ, the Son of the Blessed, or not?" And
Jesus replied, "I am." Then Jesus went even further
and commented, "and you will see the Son of Man sitting at the right hand of Power, and coming with the
clouds of heaven." This was the traditional picture of
how the Messiah would come. That was enough for the

high priest. He said, "What need have we for any further witnesses?" And turning to his associates he said, "You have heard this blasphemy. What is your decision?" And they all said, "the sentence of death."

There are curious contradictions in this story. According to official law of the Jews, no court could sit at night, nor during a religious holiday, nor for one day only. In Jewish history, no one had ever been accused of blasphemy and then sentenced to death because he claimed to be the Messiah. If a criminal was convicted of blasphemy, the Jewish officials had perfect authority to stone him to death. They did not do this, but turned Jesus over to the political authorities, who in turn had the authority only Rome had to crucify him. The episode of this hearing ends with Jesus being led into a cell in the home of the high priest and waiting there until morning, when he could be delivered to Pontius Pilate.

Whatever the curious legal complications of this hearing, the issue between the religious establishment and the religion of Jesus is very clear. When the institutional form of a religion believes it is an end in itself and therefore is concerned only about its own survival, it is already in the process of dying. Jesus said, "No religious institution is an end in itself; only God is. Put your trust in him. Put your institutions in his hands. Then you will survive; your institutions will survive."

He honored the institution, but he did not worship it. The Temple was a place for worship, so he worshipped in the Temple. The Temple was not a place to make money, so he drove out those who were making money. That is not the business of the Church. Ordered ritual and liturgical forms are perfectly natural and proper expressions for man's deep relationship of devotion to the Almighty. But the forms are not canonized in tablets of stone. They are not God; they are forms. Forms which do not change, die. God expressed his Word in a form—the form of a person. That person says, "God's concern, which overrides all other concerns, is the need of persons, what they need to live by." Those concerns take precedence over every form of ritual, worship, institutional life, and structures. "Man," he said, "is not made for the Sabbath." It is silly to think that God would make man in order that he could obey certain ritualistic acts. The ritual is meant to serve man. "If your religion," he said, "does not meet any need but your own, it is going to be destroyed. It will be destroyed just the way that temple is going to be destroyed."

Services of worship, the protection of the Holy Places of Judaism, are nothing compared to the love of God and man. Man is meant to be free to live and to love. That is why the most free man, the most loving man, walked the earth with men. Religious institutions are meant to free people, not to fetter them. People are not meant to serve the institution except as a way to serve one's neighbor and one's God.

Transpose the issues that are set forth in this hearing in Jesus' day to our day and try to identify the characters. Who are they—the Pharisees, the scribes, the priests, chief priests, ordinary priests, elders? It is pretty obvious that they are the clergy, the bishops, rectors, priests, and ministers of every denomination. They are the lawyers, especially ecclesiastical laypersons in power in churches. They are the vestries, synods, and members of church councils. It is hard to avoid the conclusion that we—not the Mafia, not the corrupt politicians, not those guilty at Watergate, not prostitutes, not drug peddlers, not makers of pornographic films— but *we* are the Pharisees.

Who are the upholders of morality and religious tradition? We are. We religious leaders are. We uphold religious tradition and we are concerned primarily with building up or saving the religious institution even when we say it is for the sake of society. We are upholders, for the most part, of traditional and conservative values. We have the responsibility for carrying on the work of the Church, doing good, buying buildings, paying bills, taking in money, spending it—largely upon ourselves.

As an Episcopalian it makes me very uneasy to recognize that the counterpart of the Jewish Sanhedrin is the General Convention of the Episcopal Church or the Diocese of Massachusetts or any other diocese, for that matter. These bodies carry on and all too often are obsessed by the business of the Church. They spend more time and money on structure and upkeep than they do on purpose and mission. They are more concerned with the business of the Church than with God's business: love of fellow men—especially those outside the church—and of him.

The trial of Jesus is in effect a trial of ourselves, only it is he who is the judge. He judges us for our preoccupation with our own internal life—issues like how shall we re-make our ritual, who shall celebrate at our altars, how shall we raise our money? It seems at times that we are so obsessed with our own lives that we forget we are meant to live for others and that the reason the Church exists is to carry out a mission for those who stand outside the Church. We are meant to be missionaries to others, and most of us are chaplains to one another.

The Christian Church is a wonderful reminder of the Sanhedrin where Christ came and where Jesus was brought before Caiaphas. In fact, it was Caiaphas who was brought before Jesus. Judgment begins in the household of God. Are not we who claim to speak in the name of Jesus—clergy, scribes, elders, priests, ecclesiastical lawyers, vestries—the ones who, more than any

other group in our society, far more than those who acknowledge themselves to be sinners in public and private, are in fact brought most sharply before Jesus? He
is not brought before us. We are brought before him.
"Who are you—the Son of God?" "Yes," he answers, "I
am." What need, therefore, have we for any further witnesses?

Jesus calls us to a new life in him as Christian men
and women. And much renewal takes place. He also
calls for the renewal of the Church. The ecclesiastical
structures are as much in need of new life, a new spirit,
as are the persons.

O Lord, renew your church—beginning
with me. Amen.

10

His Political Trial

Jesus spent that night in a cell in the home of the high priest. In the morning, after further consultation, the priests, scribes, and elders decided to turn Jesus over to Pontius Pilate, the Roman governor, with the charge that he claimed to be the King of the Jews and that, since they had no king but Caesar, Jesus should therefore be charged with the death penalty.

And as soon as it was morning the chief priests, with the elders and scribes, and the whole council held a consultation; and they bound Jesus and led him away and delivered him to Pilate. And Pilate asked him, "Are you the King of the Jews?" And he answered him, "You have said so." And the chief priests accused him of many things. And Pilate again asked him, "Have you no answer to make? See how many charges they bring against you." But Jesus made no further answer, so that Pilate wondered.

Now at the feast he used to release for them any one prisoner whom they asked. And among the rebels in prison, who had committed murder in the insurrection, there was a man called Barabbas. And the crowd came up and began to ask Pilate to do as he was wont to do for them. And he answered them, "Do you want me to release for you the King of the Jews?" For he perceived that it was out of envy that the chief priests had delivered him up. But the chief priests stirred up the crowd to have him release for them Barabbas instead. And Pilate again said to them, "Then what shall I do with the man whom you call the King of the Jews?" And they cried out again, "Crucify him." And Pilate said to them, "Why, what evil has he done?" But they shouted all the more, "Crucify him." So Pilate, wishing to satisfy the crowd, released for them Barabbas; and having scourged Jesus, he delivered him to be crucified.

And the soldiers led him away inside the palace (that is, the praetorium); and they called together the whole battalion. And they clothed him in a purple cloak, and plaiting a crown of thorns they put it on him. And when they had mocked him, they stripped him of the purple cloak, and put his own clothes on him. And they led him out to crucify him. (Mark 15:1–20)

It is interesting (and depressing because it is all too common) to note the easy abdication of religious responsibility to political authority. The Jewish leaders, in fact, had the authority to stone Jesus to death because of his blasphemy. Rather than make that decision and live with it, whatever the consequences, as mature people are meant to do—if you are mature you make your best decisions and live with them—they backed away and said, "We'll let Pilate do it. We will put pressure on him and make him put Jesus to death on political grounds. Then we will not be guilty, but he will be."

The word *religion* comes from the Latin word *religio,*

to bind together. The business of religion is the business of binding people together with one another and with God. Whatever that religion is, its concern is the relationship that binds God and men together. The Christian religion maintains that the fullest expression of that relationship is in Christ. He maintained in his teaching, in his ministry, and in himself that God's Kingdom is meant to rule the hearts and minds of men. That rule is expressed as men and women are bound together in love and as every society is built upon justice. It is as clear and as simple as that. Therefore, anything that expresses love and justice—anything, not just religious things, but any aspect of life where there is love and where justice prevails—is an expression of a religious motivation and concern. Therefore, naturally, anything that stands *against* love and justice and prevents or violates them is a matter of religious concern.

For religious forces to abdicate their responsibility to *try to determine* and therefore express what God's will is for his people, is a renunciation of what it is to be God's representatives and to claim to speak in the name of religion. I say "try to determine" because any religious interpretation is given by very fallible men and women and their political judgment may be wrong. To become a person of religious conviction does not automatically bring any insights into what is true, politically, economically, or socially. Indeed one of the perspectives of religion is to be able to see that nonreligious men are sometimes better representatives politically of God's rule than religious men.

Their basic religious concern is always, however, very simple and very all-inclusive: that *everything* that affects man affects God. Therefore, God is concerned about every aspect of man's life from the cradle to the grave, and before the cradle, the womb. It is as much God's womb as it is the woman's womb, or the man's who put the seed in the womb. For religious men to say that it is a matter of the state, is an abdication of their responsibility. What they determine to be the right life, or how they judge the termination of life in the womb, may be subject to wide disagreement and diversity, but the fact that God is there is the affirmation that God is the God of life—and, of course, death. God is God. He is to be involved in the lives of men. He is to be obeyed in every area of life where his kingdom is meant to reign. Where his kingdom reigns is wherever men and women live—the kinds of houses they live in, the kinds of houses they can't get into, the kinds of houses that decay, the kinds of houses that have rats, the kinds of schools their children go to, the kind of family life their children have, the kind of jobs they have (or don't have), and the kind of political lives they live, because all people are political animals. These are all God's. Those fundamental human issues of how men and women live together in society are finally always moral issues; as such they are God's business and therefore the business of religion as well as of politics.

Perhaps when the Gibbons of the future writes *The Decline and Fall of America* he will point out that one of the reasons for that fall was the decline in the sense of moral outrage against injustice, against corruption, against the big lie, against manipulation of opinion; and that one of the reasons for that was the abdication by America's religious forces of their responsibility to witness to "One nation under God" and their tendency to hand all decisions affecting man's life in the nation over to the state and the political leaders and to say that religion is concerned only with man's personal morality.

Religion is not simply a private matter of one's personal relationship to God—although it is that. It is a corporate matter of how citizens living together reflect the characteristics of the Kingdom of God, in some measure creating a society which makes it possible for love to be expressed and compassion to go on and undergird human affairs, for justice to be in the law courts as well as safety in the streets, for equality of opportunity, and dedication to serve the state, not to manipulate it or to ask to be served by it. A Church which abdicates its religious responsibility in these matters is a cowardly Church. A cowardly Church crucifies Christ day after day. A Church more concerned about itself than its mission, more concerned about its inner life than the life of God in the world, is a crucifying Church.

Who, then, to return to the trial, was responsble for the death of Jesus? Certainly not the Jewish people. So far as we can determine, the Jewish people—that is, the rank and file among them, the common people—in the words of one reporter, "heard Jesus gladly." They flocked around him. He was followed everywhere by crowds of ordinary citizens who, while certainly not un-derstanding who he was, knew he was someone who healed sick people, who fed hungry people, who loved little children, who called peacemakers the "blessed ones," and said that he would lay down his life for ev-erybody. Furthermore, Jesus said, "if you lay down your life for people and live in that spirit, then you have got to be able to live in a way that you never could live before." That struck a chord in the hearts of these very ordinary people. Why wouldn't the Jewish people re-spond by being glad to be in his company? No, it wasn't the Jews who were responsible for his death.

Nor was it Pilate. We like to think that if we could put our finger on the head of the state and say, "He is the guilty one," no matter what the wrongdoing, then we could be certain that justice would be done. That is never true. Pilate was not responsible. Pilate happened to be the one in office who ordered the crucifixion, but he never would have done it if the prisoner had not been delivered to him by the abdication of the religious authorities. Pilate was an administrator. His job was to keep the peace. Though, humanly speaking, it seems in those Gospel accounts that he may have wanted to save Jesus because he saw that it was for envy that the priests had delivered him, he was more concerned, as administrators usually are, to save himself and the power of his office. So he gave way finally to the pressures of the crowd that had been stirred up by the religious authorities. In order to keep the peace, he ordered Jesus' death. How ironic that it was this death and resurrection which, in a few short years, turned, as the Gospel says, "the world upside down"—Pilate's world, the world of the Romans. Pilate was weak, but neither in himself nor in his office was he responsible for the death of Jesus. It is never political office or the holders of political office who are responsible for evil, though they may give way to certain pressures. Who then is?

We often like to think that there is a special evil person who is responsible for an evil situation—like Hitler or Judas. Judas has been so identified as evil that his name has lived as the symbol of betrayal throughout human history. Why did he betray Jesus? Why, of all things, did he betray with a kiss? Why take the symbol of loyalty and turn it into the symbol of disloyalty?

Nobody knows. At least nobody knows sufficiently to present a clear case for the reason of his betrayal. Money? Not very likely. Judas had access to money. Disappointment in Jesus and the failure of his message to carry the day? Possibly, but no more than the disappointment of the other disciples. A commitment to Jesus, the conviction that he *was* the Messiah, and an impatience because he was not revealing his hand, and therefore his forcing Jesus to declare himself? That may be possible—a twisted kind of motivation which may have stemmed from the highest ideal. Nobody really knows. All we do know is that later that night he went to "his own place" and committed suicide. When we cut ourselves off, we go to our own place—and that's that.

We don't know. There is a great mystery about evil. At times we have just to accept it as a fact without understanding it. Sometimes the people who are the most evil do not understand it themselves. Some people are apparently possessed by a spirit of evil, and they can't help but do damage. They just walk through life destroying life, and they don't know what they are doing. Sometimes they do it from motivation of the highest of ideals, or so they believe. Some people, some groups of people, are simply possessed by evil.

There is no accounting sometimes for the power of evil. No accounting sometimes for what happens to friendship, for example. Friends sometimes seem possessed to destroy each other. Sometimes the greater the friendship, the greater the hate. Curious; a great mystery. Or married couples who have lived together for thirty years suddenly "uncouple," as they say. Sometimes when they uncouple they do it with a hate surpassing any human love that ever possessed them. How do you account for such viciousness between people who have loved one another, given themselves to one another, sacrificed for one another, shared life, death, birth, bed, board, defeats, victories with one another? It is a great mystery.

Sometimes all we can do is accept the fact of the Judas kiss as part of life—a kiss that we receive and a kiss, sometimes, that we give. All we can do is accept it when we receive it and then get on with life and the next thing we have to do. When we are tempted to give it, we can pass on and get on to the next thing without giving it. You generally cannot fight it any more than

Jesus could in the Garden; you can accept it and move on. In any case, we cannot accuse one evil man—Judas—of being responsible for the death of Jesus.

It is hard to avoid the conclusion that there is something in the human race—in all of us—which is really set against love and does not like it, something which will kill it if it can. We see in ourselves the same envy the priests had for position and power and prestige. They wanted to control life. We want to control life. They wanted to speak in the name of God and nobody else, and that is what we want to do. If we have something, we do not want to give it away. We certainly do not want to have it taken away. We have the same tendency to dodge responsibility that Pilate had. We do not want to be involved. We like to wash our hands of any responsibility if someone is going to get hurt and we might get blamed for it. We all know what it is like to give way to pressures the way Pilate did, to fail to speak the truth when we know it. We tend to identify with the pack we travel with. We tend, in fact, to become like other members of the pack, and therefore moral chameleons—to be one person with one pack and another person with another pack, just moving from pack to pack or place to place.

So when we look at that scene at the trial and try to put ourselves in the places of those who were carrying out the drama, we can identify with all of them. We resent love in the measure to which we are unlovable. We resist justice in the measure to which we are unjust. When the loving God comes into our life with his justice, he is unbearable; when he comes as love—pure, unadulterated, self-sacrificing love—we abhor him and we want to kill him.

But God will not stay killed. He keeps coming back. The resurrection happens day after day. No matter what we do, how much we hate, how we kill or destroy or back away from responsibilities, how we point our fingers at everybody else, God's love—God's unbearable love—is finally unbeatable. No matter how we respond or what we do or who we are, he keeps coming back gladly, persistently, gracefully, saying, "You are loved. I love you. The reality of eternity is that you are loved and will always be loved no matter what you do. I am going to keep on coming until you learn to love me."

So we can't cast stones and say, "You over there are responsible for killing Jesus." That is something that we all are responsible for because there is something in us that wants that. We confess it.

To whom then shall we turn? Look at the scene: the riled-up crowds, the frantic priests, the wavering Pilate. The only person not riled up, not frantic, not weak, is Jesus, in complete possession of himself in the middle of the tumult. He doesn't have to defend himself, or apologize for himself, or explain himself. His defense is who he is. His defense is simply his interior life, doing the will of God as he knows it. He is secure—secure in that inner integrity where he is obedient to love—the only one who not only would never kill love, but would obey it right down to his death. He had once commanded it as the rule of life and of all men in every society, and now he was to obey it. He had committed himself to accomplish the work that he had been sent to do. He is *in* God.

In our frantic, riled up, weak, wavering, fuzzy lives, to whom can we turn? He is the only one. He is the only one who has that inner resource that we know we need, and in fact, when we obey it, possess. In him we are forgiven, given peace; in him we are born to new life, borne always to the Cross, never avoiding it, finally embracing it.

If we can turn from our inner lives and move into his inner life, and with him see what it means to open ourselves to God, pressing upon him, to be obedient to love and to strive for justice, and to want above all else to do just that, then we are led into the heart of the greatest mystery of all—the heart of the mystery of God himself.

Finally, the one ultimately responsible for the crucifixion is God. *That* is the mystery. In the Cross, he expressed what was in his mind from before the beginning of the world—his unifying love for his creation, for all men, for you and for me to be at one with him. He will, in fact, in his son die to express it so that love can rise in our hearts eternally. That is the way of the Cross. And that is the way to life.

Almighty God, whose most dear son went not up to joy but first he suffered pain, and entered not into glory before he was crucified; mercifully grant that we, walking in the way of the Cross, may find it none other than the way of life and peace; through the same thy son Jesus Christ our Lord. Amen.

11

His Crucifixion

Once the scourging had taken place, the soldiers put the cross-beam over his shoulders and led him outside the city walls toward the place of crucifixion.

> And they compelled a passerby, Simon of Cyrene, who was coming in from the country, the father of Alexander and Rufus, to carry his cross. And they brought him to the place called Golgotha (which means the place of a skull). And they offered him wine mingled with myrrh; but he did not take it. And they crucified him, and divided his garments among them, casting lots for them, to decide what each should take. And it was the third hour, when they crucified him. And the inscription of the charge against him read, "The King of the Jews." And with him they crucified two robbers, one on his right and one on his left. And those who passed by derided him, wagging their heads, and saying, "Aha! You who would destroy the temple and build it in three days, save yourself, and come down from the cross!" So also the chief priests mocked him to one another with the scribes, saying "He saved others; he cannot save him-

self. Let the Christ, the King of Israel, come down now from the cross, that we may see and believe." Those who were crucified with him also reviled him.

And when the sixth hour had come, there was darkness over the whole land until the ninth hour. And at the ninth hour Jesus cried with a loud voice, "Eloi, Eloi, lama sabach-thani?" which means, "My God, my God, why hast thou forsaken me?" And some of the by-standers hearing it said, "Behold, he is calling Elijah." And one ran and, filling a sponge full of vinegar, put it on a reed and gave it to him to drink, saying, "Wait, let us see whether Elijah will come to take him down." And Jesus uttered a loud cry, and breathed his last. And the cur-tain of the temple was torn in two, from top to bottom. And when the centurion, who stood facing him, saw that he thus breathed his last, he said, "Truly this man was a son of God!"

There were also women looking on from afar, among whom were Mary Magdalene, and Mary the mother of James the younger and of Joses, and Salome. (Mark 15:21–40)

Simon's experience was not unlike that of many of you. You are just minding your business when sud-denly you have burdens pressed on you. You have re-sponsibilities thrust upon you that you had not counted on. But if you are to go on in life, you pick them up and make the best of the changed circumstances that you can. A sudden death, a reversal in fortune, a sickness, a betrayal, a disappointment—who has not had these thrust upon him, and who has not, when taken with a certain kind of spirit, found them in truth to be the way of the Cross which has led to a deeper, richer, and more satisfying life? You go on to your own Calvary and there find your crosses give you your meaning in life.

This scene on Calvary hill is the central scene of the Christian life. If you want to see what the Christian religion is in one picture, this is it. This is where eternity and reality are focused upon one scene, one picture. All other pictures embellish it or enrich it, but this *one* reflects the whole story. There is the scene, and behind the scene there is the truth that comes through it. Something comes through this which reflects the essential nature of God. He stands behind it.

In the courtyard of Trinity Church in Boston there is a statue of that great preacher, Phillips Brooks—an imposing figure in stone. Behind him with his hand on his shoulder is the figure of Jesus Christ. Brooks once wrote of the Christian life, "It is truth through personality." Through his personality and his living and preaching came the truth of Christ.

Behind the crucifixion scene is the truth of God. God himself is just behind it all, with his hand on the shoulder of Christ. God's truth shows through the personality—the person—of Jesus Christ. "And they crucified him." That is all Mark says—a simple fact. Behind that scene the truth of both God and man is revealed.

It is a revealed truth that comes when you take on those responsibilities and sufferings that are thrust upon you. Then life reveals them to you; when you carry them, you know that the truth expressed on the Cross is in fact true. It is a scene which cannot be observed; it is a scene which has to be lived.

It is not only when responsibilities are thrust upon you, but when you earnestly try to share something of the burdens of others. It may be in your family, just going a little bit further to be responsible, to lift some weight, to lighten the load, to ease the way. It may be in the community, to accept some responsibility for life and the burdens that most of its citizens carry. It may be that in your offering of your time, your energy, your money, your brains, you recognize your brother or sister under God and you want to help. That is part of the living of the Cross.

The Church at its best helps members to be members, not simply of one another, but of all men. Shared responsibilities mean some suffering shared. There is no tie that binds like shared suffering. The truth of the Cross continues to be true as we try to be true to one another, to it, and to him how stands behind it.

If the scene had a name it might be something like "The Mystery of Love"—the mystery of God and man. Who can understand it? No one except he who picks up his Cross where he is and follows him—and then never wholly.

The mystery of love is that it cannot save itself. The taunts of the priests were correct: love is not able to save itself. Christ can't come down and save himself. He is not concerned to save himself. Love is never concerned with itself, to save itself.

Christ on the Cross was there because he was obedient to love. If you are obedient to love you do not save yourself. To obey love means to renounce all power to save yourself. Christ saves you. It means to renounce all rights to protect yourself. Christ protects you. That is part of the mystery of the Cross and Christ—that he revealed the mystery of love by giving up his authority as King. And so he finally came to reign as King.

His power and his worth are seen in this: his refusal to exercise his power or to show forth his worth in any way except by love. He gave up himself.

Ever since then, whenever we have given up ourselves in love because of love, we have revealed that truth. "Vicarious suffering," it is sometimes called, on behalf of others with no return expected. That is the mystery of God and of us.

On the Cross, Christ said little (only one phrase, according to Mark) and he did nothing. What happened there was the summing up of all he had ever said and ever done. So all he had to do was accept now, take the Cross, and in the taking of it affirm love, its enduring power and mystery. That is the heart of it. It is a demonstration of love lived wholly.

This love is the last word of what it is all about. Nothing more can be said. God has said it. A mystery all around us.

It is the life of sacrifice to love. It is in the living of that mystery—our lives hidden with Christ in God—that we share the power of his resurrection. And to that we shall turn in the next chapter.

For now we are buried with Christ in his death. He lies in the tomb, hewn out of the rock. And we are hidden there with him, in him.

> The rock was made by you, God. The stone was yours. The body and the burial were yours. Grant that we may so enter into that tomb that we may be buried with Christ, and so be made partakers of his resurrection. And as partakers of you, and your love, and of your Son, may we be his body . . . living, bearing, revealing the life, the truth, and the love that is your mystery, and so live it now and always. Amen.

12

His Resurrection

We come now to the very heart of the Christian Gospel—the resurrection of Jesus Christ from the dead:

> For I delivered to you as of first importance what I also received, that Christ died for our sins in accordance with the scriptures, that he was buried, that he was raised on the third day in accordance with the scriptures, and that he appeared to Cephas, then to the twelve. Then he appeared to more than five hundred brethren at one time, most of whom are still alive, though some have fallen asleep. Then he appeared to James, then to all the apostles. Last of all, as to one untimely born, he appeared also to me. (I Corinthians 15:3–8)

His story would seem to have ended when his last breath went out of him and he was taken down from the Cross, placed in the tomb, and the rock rolled in to seal his grave forever. But the rock is rolled away and Christ appears to open the way into a new realm of existence where evil has no power, where sin is destroyed, and where the death of the physical body is of no importance because the spiritual presence of the one who inhabited that particular body endures. That new realm is both a future hope (we speak of "going to heaven" after we die) and also—and this is its significance for us—a present reality. We are now writing our earthly stories within this new realm ushered in by Christ which claims that the life of the Spirit already has power to direct our lives. We live out our own stories, then, in the light of and with the power of Jesus' story. And the whole point of his story is that death and sin do not have the power to destroy love and truth. *They* endure. And when we live them—that is, when we by faith live in Christ who is love and truth—then *we* endure. That is eternal life. And eternal life is not something to be lived after we die. It is to be lived now.

A new dimension, in other words, has come into our human existence that causes us to live differently. We are now living in a realm of existence revealed by Christ in his resurrection and through faith in him we now live it. That new dimension is living love and doing truth—being in Christ, obeying, living him. It is not so much a reality that we take on; it takes us on. We who are buried with Christ—that is, we who renounce underhanded ways to live, we who have no confidence in our own ability to lead whole lives, we who repudiate our desire to always get our own way—are by faith right now made partakers of his resurrection.

We can live risen lives now. We can participate in his being right now. We can live in his spirit right now. While we are still in the flesh we are to live in the power of his spirit. And we are dead to everything contrary to his spirit. All that egomania which has possessed our lives—How am I doing? How can I get ahead? How can I be king of the mountain?—that is all dead and gone. To live in Christ's spirit is not just a heavenly promise for by and by; it is a present reality to be lived right now.

Paul sets this new realm right before us. Though he had never seen the physical Jesus in the flesh, he knew his essential nature—his spirit. Christ, he said, "appeared to me." Well, that same Christ "appears" to us. To be literal, he also said, to be literal about everything is to kill everything because everything material finally dries up, decays and is blown away. But the spirit "brings life." That is the spirit that brings life to us right now, right here, in our earthly lives just as they are. Those lives are meant to be clothed with new life because, while we go through our earthly existence, we are at the same time walking in a new realm. That realm was brought in by Christ's resurrection from the dead.

Both realms go on at the same time. Time is measured both by our human calendar—January to December—and by God's time. Christ came to earth in the fullness of time—that is, the right time for him to live his life.

When he left this earth—and calendar time—he gave us his spirit. The spirit that was in him then moves through us now. When we who are creatures of time move through it with his spirit, then we are living in *our* fullness of time. That is, we are living as we are meant under God to live most wholly. When we appropriate Christ's spirit, then we live our lives "appropriately" for our time and our gifts. That is when we sense we are living "just right," just in the flow of things. That is to live "in grace"—gracefully.

We cannot, therefore, understand Easter in simple, chronological, literal, fleshly terms. That is a distortion of the eternal element. On the other hand, the eternal reality of Easter is meant to bear in upon us in the present.

We live chapter by chapter, and we are meant to live wholly as Christians chapter by chapter. The only chapter we've got is the present one. We run two dangers: one is the danger of living the Christian life as we knew it in the past. I was with a very distinguished widow of an exceedingly distinguished American who died twenty years ago. She didn't say a single sentence the entire evening without referring to her husband. He was dead and gone but the only reality for her was in the dead past.

We very properly need our anchors and roots, but we have to live in the present. We live in the present in different circumstances, but with the same spirit. The spirit is always the same and it is always new. And if we are touched by the spirit of the past, we can live in the same spirit continually in the present, even under drastically changed circumstances.

The other danger is our temptation always to live in the future. Our hearts are set in the future. Part of the reason is our educational system. If you get into the right nursery school, you may get into the right primary school, and you may get into the right secondary school, and then you might get into the right college or university. And then maybe you'll get a job. Our education is always pointing forward.

Young people have to make life decisions. One of the problems is that they make life decisions about what they are going to do years ahead. How are they going to live then? The question is, how are they going to live now? Young people, for example, ask "Shall I go into the ministry or not?" Nobody knows the answer to that question. The question is, can you live as a Christian person now? If you live as a Christian person now, you will be led either into the ministry or the ministry will be closed to you, and whether you go into the ministry or not is not important.

What is important is that we live in the Spirit; at the moment. That is the totality of the Spirit. That is the Spirit of the crucified and risen Christ. We can't live just with the risen Christ all by himself in the future. We can't live as though we were a spiritual body all alone. We can't be an enthusiast in the Spirit and make believe we do not have any responsibilities in this life.

The wholeness of Christ's story for the wholeness of our story is held together by the motion of the Spirit as we are able to understand the Spirit. If we take a simply literalistic interpretation of the Easter story, we are always going to be looking backwards. Our faith cannot be in the dead past. It has to be in the living Spirit. So we are set free from literalism into the fullness of the liberty of Christ's life story. That life story is the impacting together of death and life right now—not in sequence, but right now.

The resurrection of Christ, then, is directly related to our resurrection now—our being dead to sin and alive to him. We know him now by faith. And if we know him, we know him both buried and raised. We who are dead to sin are raised to new life in him, partakers of his resurrection.

> Almighty God, who through your only-begotten son Jesus Christ overcame death and opened to us the gate of everlasting life; Grant that we, who celebrate with joy the day of the Lord's resurrection, may be raised from the death of sin by your life-giving Spirit; through Jesus Christ our Lord, who lives and reigns with you and the Holy Spirit, one God, now and forever.
>
> Amen.

13

His Ascension

Do you think of heaven as a place? Or do you think of heaven as a quality of relationships? What it means to live in heaven while we are still on earth is what this chapter is all about—the Ascension of Jesus.

St. Luke describes the scene this way:

> Then he led them out as far as Bethany, and lifting up his hands, he blessed them. While he blessed them, he parted from them. And they returned to Jerusalem with great joy, and were continually in the temple blessing God. (Luke 24:50–53)

There was a time centuries ago when people could talk of a three-story universe. There was the earth where we live. Up above were the heavens. You could look up and see the stars at night and follow the sun and the moon in their courses. Then down below was an abyss where spirits lived in a kind of shadowy, insubstantial underworld.

Before Copernicus, the popular primitive understanding of eternal life was related to this three-story universe: earth where we live now, heaven above where the righteous live forever, and hell beneath for evil ones to live in torment. There was also in some medieval theology a place called purgatory below which sinners worked off their punishment for their sins and finally were rewarded by admittance into heaven, where they were re-united with their loved ones and lived with the whole company of saints praising God.

In a day where modern physics has demolished the idea of a three-story universe, it is fashionable to criticize such a simplistic structure. We are, we know now, living in an infinite, expanding universe. But old ideas die hard, and in fact symbolically there was an essential truth in thinking of eternal dimensions within an up-down, heaven-hell framework.

People thought of heaven as a place—not because the place itself was good—but because life there was good. The people were good. Christ was good. And heaven was living with those people in a loving relationship.

Hell, on the other hand, while placed beneath the earth as space where fires burned, was essentially hell because people were separated from one another and from the good, loving father.

Literalists might think of heaven and hell as places, but essentially they were words to describe relationships—heaven made up of loving relationships, and hell, an absence of relationships, each person isolated, alienated, not related to any one. To be utterly alone is hell.

Now these words are simply background to help us get to the essential nature of what the Ascension of Jesus really means. We miss the point if we think of Jesus as going up on a cloud into heaven. Symbolically that might be a helpful picture, but the real point is that he leaves this earth physically—Luke says he "parted" from his disciples—and returns to his father in his essential nature, his spirit.

It is the end of the story of Jesus Christ—on earth. It is not, however, the end of his whole story. That story goes on. As we shall see, his story is not completed. It goes on in us, and it will go on generation after generation, until the earth is no more, and shall have passed away.

But the human part of the story is completed. The actual presence of Jesus Christ on earth is now terminated. Jesus returns to his father. You might now be able to look back and say, Jesus was born to be obedient—as a son—to his father. And since God was his father, this meant being obedient to love. So you might say love was born, love went out to strengthen people, and so love suffered; since love offended people who loved only themselves, it judged them; and because people, when judged, want to strike back, they put love to death; but love by its very nature could not stop loving, so it came back to love again. But Jesus, the bearer of love, had now completed his mission—to show forth the character of love fully—so he returned to the one who had sent him, his father. Henceforth he and his father were to be one in eternity, in the heavens. The story ends, "and they both lived happily ever after."

That is why we sing the hymn:

> Alleluia! Sing to Jesus!
>   His the scepter, his the throne;
> Alleluia! his the triumph,
>   His the victory alone;
> Hark the songs of Holy Sion
>   Thunder like a mighty flood:
> Jesus out of every nation
>   Hath redeemed us by his blood."

More accurately, the father and the son and their spirit lived "happily ever after." The Ascension symbolizes the return of the inner spirit which motivated Jesus in all his actions on earth to the eternal spirit of God the father, their inner natures now perfectly merged.

We get some impression of what this means when we identify with the spirit of another. When we are so identified in the spirit of love for another, we are at one with that person even though we may be separated by a great distance. We can, in fact, "practice the presence" of that person. We can dwell in him or her. The other can dwell in us.

When that love relationship is a deep one, we can keep, we say, "in touch." And sometimes, in fact, the separation of the body makes it possible for us to go deeper in the spirit. Indeed, at certain times we can tell how the other person is in the depth of his or her being simply by looking at how we are in the depths of our being. There is a profound interplay of strength and spirit between people who love one another because there is an identity of spirit. We get re-made in the image of the other. The spirit renews, strengthens, and binds together those who share such a common spirit of love.

Moreover, death does not destroy this bond. Sometimes, in fact, it is only through death that we get deeper insight into exactly who that person was, what motivated him or her. Probably we come to the fullest knowledge of another only after death. That is knowledge that comes after the person has, so to speak, "ascended"—that is, parted from us.

So when we live by that spirit revealed to us through an earthly body, we are enabled to live more deeply the qualities of that spirit—courage, fidelity, compassion, sacrifice, outgoing concern. That spirit, we discover, never fails. Everything else seems to fail—dishonesty, self-service, greed, ego drives, obsession with self, lies. But love never fails. That is eternal.

That is the meaning of the Ascension.

We can say this in part because of our human experiences which validate it. We know from where such power for living in this way comes. When we are in deep currents of such a spirit, we are "possessed" by that spirit.

But more importantly, our experiences are validated by Christ. Our confidence is not in our experiences, but in him. It is he who gives light to illumine our experiences. Everything we go through—how we meet life, deal with failure and defeat, sin and conquer sin; how we are raised to a new life, surge through life, celebrating, exalting in it—all that is the story of his life. And since he is now "ascended," his spirit bears witness to him through our experiences. There is no place else for his spirit to go—except in and through us.

So to conclude the story of Jesus with his Ascension is but to begin the story of his spirit. As we share the spirit of the story of Jesus, we begin to participate in his eternal spirit, which he showed forth on earth and now shares with his father.

It is, then, an open-ended story. His story is not finished. It is never told except in the present. It is never told with power except in the present, that is, in our lives, in our age. It is a story, finally, which can never be simply told. It has to be believed.

It is in the living of our lives that we tell the story. We tell our stories best—reveal ourselves most fully as we really are—as we reveal Jesus' story in us. And we bring power to others to live only as we are most wholly ourselves—real, honest, authentic people, ringing true. *That* is the only power we have—our presence and, in us, Christ's presence.

He is ascended into heaven. And he lives in us on earth. Maybe it's just the other way around as well: we are already ascended into heaven, and so we can live him on earth. In either case, he and we are one in the Spirit.

> *So, Jesus ascended,*
>   *Lord of life,*
>   *Above the heavens*
>   *Reigning,*
>   *Quietly, hiddenly*
>   *Praying in us,*
> *We praise you.*
>   *Amen.*

14

His Spirit

The interview of Jesus with Nicodemus is apropos:

> Now there was a man of the Pharisees, named
> Nicodemus, a ruler of the Jews. This man came
> to Jesus by night and said to him, "Rabbi, we
> know that you are a teacher come from God; for
> no one can do these signs that you do, unless
> God is with him." Jesus answered him, "Truly,
> truly, I say to you, unless one is born anew, he
> cannot see the kingdom of God." Nicodemus
> said to him, "How can a man be born when he
> is old? Can he enter a second time into his
> mother's womb and be born?" Jesus answered,
> "Truly, truly, I say to you, unless one is born of
> water and the Spirit, he cannot enter the king-
> dom of God. That which is born of the flesh is
> flesh, and that which is born of the Spirit is
> spirit. Do not marvel that I said to you, 'You
> must be born anew.' The wind blows where it
> wills, and you hear the sound of it, but you do
> not know whence it comes or whither it goes;
> so it is with every one who is born of the Spirit.'
> (John 3:1–8)

The word *spirit,* in its most fundamental sense, is the same as the word *breath.* While you are breathing you are alive. When you stop breathing you are dead.

Christ has sent his spirit to "breathe through" his people so they might be dead to sin and alive to righteousness—that is, so they might live fully, wholly, completely as the unique person each is meant to be, and that means to live fully, wholly, completely in him. When you are filled with his spirit, you can not only take anything in life, you can turn the worst into the best and live in a celebrating, affirming, glorifying kind of way.

So it is important to be in touch first of all with your own spirit, for as it has been said, "the spirit of man is the candle of the Lord, searching all the inward parts." You try to sense your own spirit. What makes up that distinctive, unique "you" which sets you apart from every other human being and which, when you can identify it, makes it possible for you to be truly yourself? That sense of your own spirit rises within you when you are quiet, centered, and eager simply to wait for it to express itself.

The poet Rainer Maria Rilke describes the process as he tries to help a young aspiring poet to identify this spirit within himself. "The necessary thing," he writes, ". . . is after all but this . . . solitude, great inner solitude, going into oneself and for hours meeting no one. This, one must be able to attain. . . . Be attentive to that which rises up in you, and set it above everything that you observe about you. You must not be frightened if a sadness rises up within you. You must think that something is happening to you, that life has not forgotten you, that it holds you in its hands . . . it will not let you fall."

Christians believe that the "something" that is happening is the Spirit happening. The Spirit has not forgotten us. He holds us in his hands. He will not let us fall. When we pray, we pray that God's Spirit simply will confirm us in ourselves, strengthening us to be ourselves, our complete whole selves in him.

Now the Spirit, Jesus reminds us in his conversations with Nicodemus, has a mind of its own. It blows where it will. No human being controls the direction of the Spirit nor determines upon whom it will breathe. God does that.

So the Spirit, then, has his own mind for us, his own intention, his own purpose. He is, to put it another way, "his own." He is not ours. We do not possess him or own him. He possesses us, owns us. He comes upon us, rises up within us, quietly; gradually we come to see him and what he is doing. Or, it may be, he overwhelms us, "zaps" us—and in the twinkling of an eye we know we belong to him, are converted. But in either case, or in any case, the Spirit is God's and comes from God. He is the *initiator*.

When I sense the Spirit, I sense it is coming from beyond me, from God. He initiates the relationship. He seeks us. It is always a personal search. All we need do is be quiet and alert to sense his searching for us by touching our spirit. So we go within. We are *deepened*. We deliberately descend into the depths, unafraid to explore the depths of oneself. There in the inner exploration one begins to explore God—the two seem to merge. You may remember that passage from *Markings* where Dag Hammarskjold wrote:

> . . . you are *one* in God, and God is wholly in you.
> just as, for you, He is wholly in all,
> With this faith, in prayer you descend into your-
>   self to meet the other,
> in the steadfastness and light of this union,

see that all things stand, like yourelf, alone before God . . .

In the faith which is God's marriage to the soul,
everything, therefore, has a meaning.
So live, then, that you may use what has been
put into your hand . . . *

This is what a deepened self is about: where you go
within to discover Christ with whom your life is hidden
in God.

This sense of the self in Christ being identified by the
Spirit means, on the one hand, a renewing of the self—
becoming more of a whole person, your own self, so you
can say, "I am discovering my self. I am becoming
somebody." And on the other hand it means a going out
to others, an affirming of others, a strengthening of
others, caring for them. Christianity as caring is one of
the essential notes in the Christian life.

That is another way of saying, God is known through
relationships. He bears in upon us through relationships. God the father expressed his spirit through
his son, and when his son left us, he sent his spirit to
bind us—all creation—together. While we sense the
Spirit most easily in the loving, caring relationships of
life—and are called to express those qualities in our
lives—he comes through *all* relationships, the bruising
and breaking ones, as well as the reconciling ones. "In
the faith," Hammarskjold writes, "which is God's marriage to the soul *everything* therefore has a meaning."

The Spirit speaks therefore in the cries of the hungry,
in the outrage of the dispossessed and discriminated
against, in the wailing of the bereaved. The Spirit

*Dag Hammarskjold, *Markings* (New York: Alfred A. Knopf, Inc., 1973), p.
165.

groans and travails through the pain and injustice of God's creation broken, calling his creatures to put it back together again; to drive toward justice, to renew a social order where injustice is so painful. Who cries? Christ cries.

So to refer to the Spirit in personal, individual terms only and not to listen to him in the social, corporate structures of life is in fact to block our ears to him. The Spirit is experienced not only in a *deepened* life, but in a *shared* life—shared with all creation.

The final reflection is simply that where we experience the Spirit—in whatever relationship, whatever experience—we experience Christ. He holds everything together; that is, love holds everything together. In a broken world where injustice and evil prevail, this means that the Cross holds everything together. Built right into the structure of existence is this agony of the Cross—love's Spirit obeying love and being crucified— and of course also, at the same time, the joy of the Cross. Pain and joy are bound together, embedded in the heart of the mystery of existence, bound by the Spirit, giving meaning to its mystery.

Therefore there is hope—the hope of glory.

> . . . of which I became a minister according to the divine office which was given to me for you, to make the word of God fully known . . . (Colossians 1:25)

The mystery, hidden for ages and generations, is now made manifest as God through his spirit has made known to those whom he has chosen how great are the riches of this mystery, which is Christ in you, the hope of glory.

This life—our individual deepened life, our shared life—is the Christ life. It is Christ. It is our life hidden

with Christ in God. It is Christ's life hidden in us in the
mystery of life, in God.

Therefore, since we have sensed the Spirit and want
to live our personal lives uniquely in the Spirit, all we
need do—God will do it for us as we live in him—is
show forth the fruit of the Spirit. The fruit of the Spirit
is love, joy, peace, patience, kindness, goodness, faith-
fulness, gentleness, self-control.

So let us pray that such a life in the Spirit may truly
be ours.

> The wind blows, God, just like your
> spirit. It comes and goes any way you want
> it to because it is yours. It is your breath,
> and nobody owns it except you.

> We can wait for it. Be patient, expectant,
> hopeful, prepared for it. And we do this best
> as we are patient with one another, love
> one another, have peace and joy in our
> hearts, are kind and good, faithful and gen-
> tle and control ourselves.

> So as you give us that disposition of
> yours, we pray that we may receive your
> spirit more and more, until we come unto
> your heavenly kingdom. Amen.

15

His Church

Do you distinguish between going to church and being the Church? Can you be a good Christian without going to church? What difference does going to church make for your Christian life? What difference does the Church make? These are the questions we should consider.

The earliest description we have of the Church in the New Testament is in the Acts of the Apostles. The author describes what the first Christians did after they had heard Peter explain the essential nature of their belief. Their conviction was, he said, that Jesus of Nazareth, who had been crucified, had been raised from the dead by God who made him both Lord and Christ. Then those who received this Word, accepted it, were baptized, and then this is what they did:

> They devoted themselves to the apostles' teaching and fellowship, to the breaking of bread and the prayers. (Acts 2:42).

Ever since then Christians have said, "to share this life, this Christian life, makes all the difference in the world." Do you think it does? Do you see any evidence that to belong to the Church makes any difference at all? What is the case for the Church?

The case for the Church is: that is where the story of Jesus is told, that is where the story of Jesus is best lived; and it is within the company of Christian people that you can write your own story—the story of the meaning of your life and its significance—better than anywhere else. The claim of the Church is that if you really want your life to count for something, it will count for most if it is directly related to the life of Christ. If you take his life and death and resurrection seriously—that is, if you appropriate his spirit, expressed in his life—you will have a sense of meaning and of joy, and of really counting for something that will be more powerful than any other kind of life you can lead. It will mean more to yourself; it will mean more to the people who are associated with you in your life, and it will mean more to the society of which you are a part. Our society needs people who are rooted and grounded in love, compassion, sacrifice, and integrity, and who are committed to work for justice in the land, because only so can they love their neighbors as themselves. It is the role of the state to execute justice. And it is the citizens of the nation who know they are also citizens of God's Kingdom of righteousness who can help bring this to pass.

That means ordinary citizens like you and me, who are just trying to write the story of our lives in some significant way. That is why I have tried in this book to relate the story of Jesus to our story. We write our story best when we write in the light of Jesus' story. Let me put this even more strongly: Christians believe that we write our individual, personal stories best when we let Jesus write them with us. Our story is his story. His story is continuing to be written in the lives of each of us. It is the story of Jesus and his love. It is the story of

God the creator of the universe come to earth to live in Jesus, who overcame all the evil in the world, including death, and who has given his spirit to those who live by faith, so the whole world can see the nature of his love. That is the reason the Church exists. It is to show the character of the power that lies beneath and behind the mystery of human existence as love, and it does so as its members promote justice, peace and love and continually point to that person, Jesus Christ, who lived God's nature completely.

So if you want to count for something, can you think of anything that means anything more than this for our world? What more does the world need than people committed to love and justice, to feed the hungry, to break down weapons that destroy, to build peace and mutual good-will, to stand firm against oppression and to proclaim that in the human family, we are all members one of another, meant to strengthen one another.

Some of you know this and are living members of the Church. Others of you don't know it, but would like to believe it and belong. And some of you undoubtedly don't believe it and don't want to belong.

Let me add two concluding thoughts. The first is to confess that the Church—the institutional Church I am talking of—is not what she is meant to be nor what Christ wants her to be. She is usually concerned with herself and matters that affect only her own inner life, and not sufficiently concerned about her missions, nor the condition of those who stand outside her life, especially the poor and the dispossessed, those cut out of the mainstream of American life. Much of her life is trivial, the matters that engage her attention not worth that attention. She has the resulting sin of being more concerned with herself than her Lord and his life. Any churchperson who knows anything knows that the case for the Church can be presented only after this first word of confession and repentance, and that she is not what she ought to be.

And the second word is this. It is a word that has been spoken many times in this book. It is that the stories of our lives are written by ourselves. We can't blame anybody else because our lives don't work out the way we want them to. We have to make our decisions about the direction of our lives and then we have to live with those decisions. That is what mature people do. Mature Christian people make those decisions with Christ, in his spirit, for his purposes. They wait upon him in every decision in order that they may know his will, and then in faith with his power, do it. That is Christian living. That is how we write our stories; it is how he continues to write his story in us.

Exactly the same steps are taken with regard to the Church. Nobody is going to change the Church except the people of the Church. And they are going to change it by the quality of their lives. When the spirit of Christ is welcomed into their hearts and minds and they are determined to live henceforth, not for themselves but for him, then power will be from on high to renew, reform, empower the Church. The new day for the Church rises from the new day of Christians living the story of their lives together with the living story of Jesus and his love.

It lies in the gathering together of people who know that Christ is their Lord and also the Lord of all peoples, including those who never heard of him. In that company so gathered, there is both the meeting of one another and the meeting of Christ. As they accept and love each other, they accept and love Christ. In the breaking of bread, they are fed by the Spirit of him who was broken for the unity of the world and all the peoples in it with one another and with God. And since he has been raised from the dead, they share in the power of his resurrection, and live in his spirit. The prayers they offer are prayers for the world and for themselves. Those prayers are Christ's prayers. He is praying through them and offering himself and them to his heavenly father that all may be one in him.

Do you want to help? Do you want to be part of this? Do you want to have your life count in this way?

There is one way. Write the story of your life in a way that is consistent with your unique spirit. Then as you go within to touch that spirit, offer it to Christ. Ask him to send his spirit so that, merged with yours, he and you may write the story of your life—and so it may be his. That is living!

And that is living in Christ's Church!

> *Almighty God,*
> *in Christ's love*
> *you are one*
> *in us and we in you.*
>
> *By your Spirit*
> *may we live our stories*
> *as Jesus' story*
> *and so take our part*
> *in redeeming the world*
> *today—for your love's sake.*
> *Amen.*